Just The

facts101
Textbook Key Facts

CW01498531

Textbook Outlines, Highlights, and Practice Quizzes

Jonas And Kovner's Health Care Delivery In The United States

by Anthony R. Kovner, 11 Edition

Title Page

facts101
LEARNING SYSTEM

"Just the Facts101" is a Content Technologies publication and tool designed to give you all the facts from your textbooks. Register for the full practice test for each of your chapters for virtually any of your textbooks.

Facts101 has built custom study tools specific to your textbook. We provide all of the factual testable information and unlike traditional study guides, we will never send you back to your textbook for more information.

YOU WILL NEVER HAVE TO HIGHLIGHT A BOOK AGAIN!

Facts101 StudyGuides

All of the information in this StudyGuide is written specifically for your textbook. We include the key terms, places, people, and concepts... the information you can expect on your next exam!

Facts101

Only Facts101 gives you the outlines, highlights, and PRACTICE TESTS specific to your textbook. Facts101 sister Cram101.com is an online application where you'll discover study tools designed to make the most of your limited study time.

www.Cram101.com

STUDYING MADE EASY

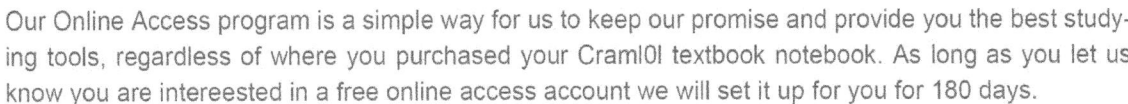

This Cram101 notebook is designed to make studying easier and increase your comprehension of the textbook material. Instead of starting with a blank notebook and trying to write down everything discussed in class lectures, you can use this Cram101 textbook notebook and annotate your notes along with the lecture.

Our goal is to give you the best tools for success.

For a supreme understanding of the course, pair your notebook with our online tools at www.cram101.com

Our Online Access program is a simple way for us to keep our promise and provide you the best studying tools, regardless of where you purchased your Cram101 textbook notebook. As long as you let us know you are intereested in a free online access account we will set it up for you for 180 days.

Online Access:

SIMPLE STEPS TO GET A FREE ACCOUNT:

Email Travis.Reese@cram101.com

Include:

Order number

ISBN of Guide

Retailer where purchased

Jonas And Kovner's Health Care Delivery In The United States
Anthony R. Kovner, 11

CONTENTS

1. THE CHALLENGE OF HEALTH CARE DELIVERY AND HEALTH POLICY 5
2. A VISUAL OVERVIEW OF HEALTH CARE DELIVERY IN THE UNITED STATES 12
3. GOVERNMENT AND HEALTH INSURANCE: THE POLICY PROCESS 19
4. COMPARATIVE HEALTH SYSTEMS 27
5. POPULATION HEALTH 38
6. PUBLIC HEALTH: A TRANSFORMATION FOR THE 21ST CENTURY 48
7. HEALTH AND BEHAVIOR 60
8. VULNERABLE POPULATIONS: A TALE OF TWO NATIONS 73
9. ORGANIZATION OF CARE 89
10. THE HEALTH WORKFORCE 106
11. HEALTH CARE FINANCING 114
12. HEALTH CARE COSTS AND VALUE 127
13. HIGH-QUALITY HEALTH CARE 137
14. MANAGING AND GOVERNING HEALTH CARE ORGANIZATIONS 148
15. HEALTH INFORMATION TECHNOLOGY 157
16. THE FUTURE OF HEALTH CARE DELIVERY AND HEALTH POLICY 168

1. THE CHALLENGE OF HEALTH CARE DELIVERY AND HEALTH POLICY

CHAPTER OUTLINE: KEY TERMS, PEOPLE, PLACES, CONCEPTS

	Health
	Fertility clinic
	Resource-based relative value scale
	Waterlow score
	Service
	Health care
	Environmental enrichment
	Environmental protection
	Quality improvement
	Outcome
	Whitehall Study
	Catastrophic
	Consumer
	Motivation
	Policy
	Case study

1. THE CHALLENGE OF HEALTH CARE DELIVERY AND HEALTH POLICY

Health	Health is the level of functional or metabolic efficiency of a living being. In humans, it is the general condition of a person's mind and body, usually meaning to be free from illness, injury or pain (as in 'good health' or 'healthy'). The World Health Organization (WHO) defined health in its broader sense in 1946 as 'a state of complete physical, mental, and social well-being and not merely the absence of disease or infirmity.' Although this definition has been subject to controversy, in particular as lacking operational value and because of the problem created by use of the word 'complete', it remains the most enduring .
Fertility clinic	Fertility clinics are staffed medical clinics that assist couples, and , who want to become parents but for medical reasons have been unable to achieve this goal via the natural course. Clinics apply a number of tests and sometimes very advanced medical procedures to obtain the desired conceptions and pregnancies. For the male, semen collection is a standard diagnostic test to ascertain problems with the semen quality.
Resource-based relative value scale	Resource-based relative value scale is a schema used to determine how much money medical providers should be paid. It is partially used by Medicare in the United States and by nearly all Health maintenance organizations (HMOs). Resource based relative value scale assigns procedures performed by a physician or other medical provider a relative value which is adjusted by geographic region (so a procedure performed in Manhattan is worth more than a procedure performed in Dallas).
Waterlow score	The 'Waterlow score gives an estimated risk of a patient developing a pressure sore. It is named after Judy Waterlow.
Service	In economics, a service is an intangible commodity. More specifically, services are an intangible equivalent of economic goods. Service provision is often an economic activity where the buyer does not generally, except by exclusive contract, obtain exclusive ownership of the thing purchased.
Health care	Health care is the diagnosis, treatment, and prevention of disease, illness, injury, and other physical and mental impairments in humans. Health care is delivered by practitioners in medicine, chiropractic, dentistry, nursing, pharmacy, allied health, and other care providers. It refers to the work done in providing primary care, secondary care and tertiary care, as well as in public health.
Environmental enrichment	Environmental enrichment concerns how the brain is affected by the stimulation of its information processing provided by its surroundings (including the opportunity to interact socially). Brains in richer, more stimulating environments, have increased numbers of synapses, and the dendrite arbors upon which they reside are more complex.

Environmental protection	Environmental protection is a practice of protecting the natural environment on individual, organizational or governmental levels, for the benefit of the natural environment and humans. Due to the pressures of population and technology, the biophysical environment is being degraded, sometimes permanently. This has been recognized, and governments have begun placing restraints on activities that cause environmental degradation.
Quality improvement	The term quality management has a specific meaning within many business sectors. This specific definition, which does not aim to assure 'good quality' by the more general definition, but rather to ensure that an organization or product is consistent, can be considered to have four main components: quality planning, quality control, quality assurance and quality improvement. Quality management is focused not only on product/service quality, but also the means to achieve it.
Outcome	In game theory, an outcome is a set of moves or strategies taken by the players, or it is their payoffs resulting from the actions or strategies taken by all players. The two are complementary in that, given knowledge of the set of strategies of all players, the final state of the game is known, as are any relevant payoffs. In a game where chance or a random event is involved, the outcome is not known from only the set of strategies, but is only realized when the random event(s) are realized.
Whitehall Study	The original Whitehall Study investigated social determinants of health, specifically the cardiorespiratory disease prevalence and mortality rates among British male civil servants between the ages of 20 and 64. The initial prospective cohort study, the Whitehall I Study, examined over 18,000 male civil servants, and was conducted over a period of ten years, beginning in 1967. A second cohort study, the Whitehall II Study, examined the health of 10,308 civil servants aged 35 to 55, of whom two thirds were men and one third women. The response rate for Whitehall II was 73% in total, 74% for men and 71% for women. A long-term follow-up of study subjects from the first two phases is ongoing.
Catastrophic	A catastrophe is an extremely large-scale disaster, a horrible event. It may also refer to: · Catastrophe bond, a risk-linked security used to share risks with bond investors · Catastrophe (book), a non-fiction book by Dick Morris and Eileen McGann · Catastrophe (drama), the climax and resolution of a plot in ancient Greek drama and poems · Catastrophe modeling, in Insurance, projecting of the cost of losses due to a catastrophic event · Catastrophe , a 1982 short play by Samuel Beckett · Catastrophe theory, a field of mathematics that studies how the behavior of dynamic systems can change drastically with small variations · Microtubular catastrophe, a feature of the cytoskeleton in eukaryotic cells · Catastrophe (TV series), a five-part science series on Channel 4 a bridge collapses) · catastrophic, a difficulty rating in Dance Dance Revolution

1. THE CHALLENGE OF HEALTH CARE DELIVERY AND HEALTH POLICY

Consumer	Consumers are organisms of an ecological food chain that receive their energy by consuming other organisms. These organisms are formally referred to as heterotrophs, which includes animals, bacteria and fungus. Such organisms may consume by various means, including predation, parasitization, and biodegradation.
Motivation	Motivation is the activation or energization of goal-oriented behavior. motivation may be intrinsic or extrinsic. The term is generally used for humans but, theoretically, it can also be used to describe the causes for animal behavior as well.
Policy	A policy is typically described as a principle or rule to guide decisions and achieve rational outcomes. The term is not normally used to denote what is actually done, this is normally referred to as either procedure or protocol. Policies are generally adopted by the Board of or senior governance body within an organization whereas procedures or protocols would be developed and adopted by senior executive officers.
Case study	A case study is an intensive analysis of an individual unit (e.g., a person, group, or event) stressing developmental factors in relation to context. The case study is common in social sciences and life sciences. Case studies may be descriptive or explanatory.

1. _____s are staffed medical clinics that assist couples, and , who want to become parents but for medical reasons have been unable to achieve this goal via the natural course. Clinics apply a number of tests and sometimes very advanced medical procedures to obtain the desired conceptions and pregnancies.

   For the male, semen collection is a standard diagnostic test to ascertain problems with the semen quality.

   a. transillumination
   b. Drawer test
   c. Fertility clinic
   d. Loop electrosurgical excision procedure

2. . _____ is the diagnosis, treatment, and prevention of disease, illness, injury, and other physical and mental impairments in humans. _____ is delivered by practitioners in medicine, chiropractic, dentistry, nursing, pharmacy, allied health, and other care providers. It refers to the work done in providing primary care, secondary care and tertiary care, as well as in public health.

   a. Health care

   b. NHS primary care trust

   c. Primary care physician

   d. Primary care

3. _____ is the level of functional or metabolic efficiency of a living being. In humans, it is the general condition of a person's mind and body, usually meaning to be free from illness, injury or pain (as in 'good _____' or 'healthy'). The World _____ Organization (WHO) defined _____ in its broader sense in 1946 as 'a state of complete physical, mental, and social well-being and not merely the absence of disease or infirmity.' Although this definition has been subject to controversy, in particular as lacking operational value and because of the problem created by use of the word 'complete', it remains the most enduring .

   a. Sano Sansar Initiative

   b. Sex differences in medicine

   c. Health

   d. mortality ratio

4. _____ is a schema used to determine how much money medical providers should be paid. It is partially used by Medicare in the United States and by nearly all Health maintenance organizations (HMOs).

   Resource based relative value scale assigns procedures performed by a physician or other medical provider a relative value which is adjusted by geographic region (so a procedure performed in Manhattan is worth more than a procedure performed in Dallas).

   a. Retiree Drug Subsidy

   b. Resource-based relative value scale

   c. Stark Law

   d. Supplemental needs trust

5. In game theory, an _____ is a set of moves or strategies taken by the players, or it is their payoffs resulting from the actions or strategies taken by all players. The two are complementary in that, given knowledge of the set of strategies of all players, the final state of the game is known, as are any relevant payoffs. In a game where chance or a random event is involved, the _____ is not known from only the set of strategies, but is only realized when the random event(s) are realized.

   a. Ultimatum game

   b. Unbeatable strategy

   c. Outcome

   d. Uniform price auction

ANSWER KEY
1. THE CHALLENGE OF HEALTH CARE DELIVERY AND HEALTH POLICY

1. c
2. a
3. c
4. b
5. c

You can take the complete Online Interactive Chapter Practice Test

for 1. THE CHALLENGE OF HEALTH CARE DELIVERY AND HEALTH POLICY
on all key terms, persons, places, and concepts.

No Additional Costs

http://www.Cram101.com

Register, send an email request to Travis.Reese@Cram101.com to get your user Id and password.

Include your customer order number, and ISBN number from your studyguide Retailer.

2. A VISUAL OVERVIEW OF HEALTH CARE DELIVERY IN THE UNITED STAT

CHAPTER OUTLINE: KEY TERMS, PEOPLE, PLACES, CONCEPTS

	Consumer
	Perception
	Group Health
	Health
	Initiative
	Policy
	Environmental enrichment
	Environmental protection
	Gross domestic product
	Health care
	Institution
	Population health
	Coalition
	Copayment
	Outcome
	Underinsurance
	Quality improvement

Consumer	Consumers are organisms of an ecological food chain that receive their energy by consuming other organisms. These organisms are formally referred to as heterotrophs, which includes animals, bacteria and fungus. Such organisms may consume by various means, including predation, parasitization, and biodegradation.
Perception	In psychology and the cognitive sciences, perception is the process of acquiring, interpreting, selecting, and organizing sensory information.
Group Health	Group Health Cooperative, more commonly known as Group Health, is a Seattle, Washington based nonprofit healthcare organization. Established in 1945, it today provides coverage and care for about 700,000 people in Washington and Idaho and is one of the largest private employers in Washington. Patients who receive care at its medical centers are provided Web access to their medical records, secure emailing with doctors and nurses and the ability to fill prescriptions online that are mailed to homes without a shipping charge.
Health	Health is the level of functional or metabolic efficiency of a living being. In humans, it is the general condition of a person's mind and body, usually meaning to be free from illness, injury or pain (as in 'good health' or 'healthy'). The World Health Organization (WHO) defined health in its broader sense in 1946 as 'a state of complete physical, mental, and social well-being and not merely the absence of disease or infirmity.' Although this definition has been subject to controversy, in particular as lacking operational value and because of the problem created by use of the word 'complete', it remains the most enduring .
Initiative	An initiative represents an enterprise's readiness to embark on a new venture. Generally speaking, the motivation for an initiative arises from a desire to accomplish something that would benefit the enterprise, such as improving productivity, reducing costs or increasing market share.
	A typical initiative is expressed as a process and includes metrics and time frames.
Policy	A policy is typically described as a principle or rule to guide decisions and achieve rational outcomes. The term is not normally used to denote what is actually done, this is normally referred to as either procedure or protocol. Policies are generally adopted by the Board of or senior governance body within an organization whereas procedures or protocols would be developed and adopted by senior executive officers.
Environmental enrichment	Environmental enrichment concerns how the brain is affected by the stimulation of its information processing provided by its surroundings (including the opportunity to interact socially). Brains in richer, more stimulating environments, have increased numbers of synapses, and the dendrite arbors upon which they reside are more complex. This effect happens particularly during neurodevelopment, but also to a lesser degree in adulthood.

2. A VISUAL OVERVIEW OF HEALTH CARE DELIVERY IN THE UNITED STATES

Environmental protection	Environmental protection is a practice of protecting the natural environment on individual, organizational or governmental levels, for the benefit of the natural environment and humans. Due to the pressures of population and technology, the biophysical environment is being degraded, sometimes permanently. This has been recognized, and governments have begun placing restraints on activities that cause environmental degradation.
Gross domestic product	Gross domestic product is the market value of all officially recognized final goods and services produced within a country in a year, or other given period of time. gross domestic product per capita is often considered an indicator of a country's standard of living. gross domestic product per capita is not a measure of personal income .
Health care	Health care is the diagnosis, treatment, and prevention of disease, illness, injury, and other physical and mental impairments in humans. Health care is delivered by practitioners in medicine, chiropractic, dentistry, nursing, pharmacy, allied health, and other care providers. It refers to the work done in providing primary care, secondary care and tertiary care, as well as in public health.
Institution	An institution is any structure or mechanism of social order and cooperation governing the behavior of a set of individuals within a given human community. Institutions are identified with a social purpose and permanence, transcending individual human lives and intention by enforcing rules that governs cooperative human behavior. The term 'institution' is commonly applied to customs and behavior patterns important to a society, as well as to particular formal organizations of government and public service.
Population health	Population health has been defined as 'the health outcomes of a group of individuals, including the distribution of such outcomes within the group.' It is an approach to health that aims to improve the health of an entire population. One major step in achieving this aim is to reduce health inequities among population groups. Population health seeks to step beyond the individual-level focus of mainstream medicine and public health by addressing a broad range of factors that impact health on a population-level, such as environment, social structure, resource distribution, etc.
Coalition	A coalition is an alliance among individuals or groups, during which they cooperate in joint action, each in his own self-interest, joining forces together for a common cause. This alliance may be temporary or a matter of convenience. A coalition thus differs from a more formal covenant.
Copayment	In the United States, copayment is accessed. It is technically a form of coinsurance, but is defined differently in health insurance where a coinsurance is a percentage payment after the deductible up to a certain limit. It must be paid before any policy benefit is payable by an insurance company.
Outcome	In game theory, an outcome is a set of moves or strategies taken by the players, or it is their payoffs resulting from the actions or strategies taken by all players.

The two are complementary in that, given knowledge of the set of strategies of all players, the final state of the game is known, as are any relevant payoffs. In a game where chance or a random event is involved, the outcome is not known from only the set of strategies, but is only realized when the random event(s) are realized.

Underinsurance	Condition of average (also called underinsurance in the U.S., or principal of average, subject to average, or pro rata condition of average in Commonwealth countries) is the insurance term used when calculating a payout against a claim where the policy undervalues the sum insured. In the event of partial loss, the amount paid against a claim will be in the same proportion as the value of the underinsurance.
	The formula used is
	where Payout is the amount paid out by the policy, Claim is the amount claimed against the policy after a loss, Sum Insured is the maximum amount to be paid out by the policy, and Current Value is the value the policy should be insured for.
Quality improvement	The term quality management has a specific meaning within many business sectors. This specific definition, which does not aim to assure 'good quality' by the more general definition, but rather to ensure that an organization or product is consistent, can be considered to have four main components: quality planning, quality control, quality assurance and quality improvement. Quality management is focused not only on product/service quality, but also the means to achieve it.

CHAPTER QUIZ: KEY TERMS, PEOPLE, PLACES, CONCEPTS

1. In game theory, an _____ is a set of moves or strategies taken by the players, or it is their payoffs resulting from the actions or strategies taken by all players. The two are complementary in that, given knowledge of the set of strategies of all players, the final state of the game is known, as are any relevant payoffs. In a game where chance or a random event is involved, the _____ is not known from only the set of strategies, but is only realized when the random event(s) are realized.

    a. Outcome
    b. Unbeatable strategy
    c. Uncorrelated asymmetry
    d. Uniform price auction

2. . A _____ is an alliance among individuals or groups, during which they cooperate in joint action, each in his own self-interest, joining forces together for a common cause. This alliance may be temporary or a matter of convenience. A _____ thus differs from a more formal covenant.

a. 19NorDehydroepiandrosterone
b. Coalition
c. Public health
d. Public health insurance option

3. A _____ is typically described as a principle or rule to guide decisions and achieve rational outcomes. The term is not normally used to denote what is actually done, this is normally referred to as either procedure or protocol. _____(ies) are generally adopted by the Board of or senior governance body within an organization whereas procedures or protocols would be developed and adopted by senior executive officers.

a. Policy
b. Polynomial conjoint measurement
c. Predispositioning theory
d. Price of stability

4. _____ is the diagnosis, treatment, and prevention of disease, illness, injury, and other physical and mental impairments in humans. _____ is delivered by practitioners in medicine, chiropractic, dentistry, nursing, pharmacy, allied health, and other care providers. It refers to the work done in providing primary care, secondary care and tertiary care, as well as in public health.

a. Health care
b. NHS primary care trust
c. Primary care physician
d. Primary care

5. _____ is the market value of all officially recognized final goods and services produced within a country in a year, or other given period of time. _____ per capita is often considered an indicator of a country's standard of living.

_____ per capita is not a measure of personal income .

a. Gross domestic product
b. action plan
c. 2 mile
d. Est: Playing the Game

1. a

2. b

3. a

4. a

5. a

You can take the complete Online Interactive Chapter Practice Test

for 2. A VISUAL OVERVIEW OF HEALTH CARE DELIVERY IN THE UNITED STATES
on all key terms, persons, places, and concepts.

No Additional Costs

http://www.Cram101.com

Register, send an email request to Travis.Reese@Cram101.com to get your user Id and password.

Include your customer order number, and ISBN number from your studyguide Retailer.

3. GOVERNMENT AND HEALTH INSURANCE: THE POLICY PROCESS

CHAPTER OUTLINE: KEY TERMS, PEOPLE, PLACES, CONCEPTS

_____ Medicare

_____ Welfare

_____ Alternative medicine

_____ Health

_____ Service

_____ Income

_____ Health insurance

_____ Medicaid

_____ Cranial root of accessory nerve

_____ Health insurance coverage in the United States

_____ Copayment

_____ Institution

_____ Policy

_____ Process

_____ Catastrophic

_____ Long-term care

_____ Nurse Practitioner

_____ Case study

3. GOVERNMENT AND HEALTH INSURANCE: THE POLICY PROCESS

Medicare	Medicare is the unofficial name for Canada's publicly funded universal health insurance system. The formal terminology for the insurance system is provided by the Canada Health Act and the health insurance legislation of the individual provinces and territories. Under the terms of the Canada Health Act, all 'insured persons' (basically, legal residents of Canada, including permanent residents) are entitled to receive 'insured services' without copayment.
Welfare	Welfare is a type of financial or other aid provided to people in need and can take many forms in various countries or contexts. In most developed countries, it is largely provided by the government. It may also be organized by charities; informal social groups; religious groups; or inter-governmental organizations such as the United Nations.
Alternative medicine	Alternative medicine is any practice claiming to heal 'that does not fall within the realm of conventional medicine.' It may be based on historical or cultural traditions, rather than on scientific evidence. Alternative medicine is frequently grouped with complementary medicine or integrative medicine, which, in general, refers to the same interventions when used in conjunction with mainstream techniques, under the umbrella term complementary and alternative medicine, or CAM. Critics maintain that the terms 'complementary' and 'alternative medicine' are deceptive euphemisms meant to give an impression of medical authority. A 1998 systematic review of studies assessing its prevalence in 13 countries concluded that about 31% of cancer patients use some form of complementary and alternative medicine.
Health	Health is the level of functional or metabolic efficiency of a living being. In humans, it is the general condition of a person's mind and body, usually meaning to be free from illness, injury or pain (as in 'good health' or 'healthy'). The World Health Organization (WHO) defined health in its broader sense in 1946 as 'a state of complete physical, mental, and social well-being and not merely the absence of disease or infirmity.' Although this definition has been subject to controversy, in particular as lacking operational value and because of the problem created by use of the word 'complete', it remains the most enduring .
Service	In economics, a service is an intangible commodity. More specifically, services are an intangible equivalent of economic goods. Service provision is often an economic activity where the buyer does not generally, except by exclusive contract, obtain exclusive ownership of the thing purchased.
Income	Income is the consumption and savings opportunity gained by an entity within a specified timeframe, which is generally expressed in monetary terms.

	However, for households and individuals, 'income is the sum of all the wages, salaries, profits, interests payments, rents and other forms of earnings received... in a given period of time.'
	In the field of public economics, the term may refer to the accumulation of both monetary and non-monetary consumption ability, with the former (monetary) being used as a proxy for total income. Increase in income
	Income per capita has been increasing steadily in almost every country.
Health insurance	Health insurance is insurance against the risk of incurring medical expenses among individuals. By estimating the overall risk of health care and health system expenses among a targeted group, an insurer can develop a routine finance structure, such as a monthly premium or payroll tax, to ensure that money is available to pay for the health care benefits specified in the insurance agreement. The benefit is administered by a central organization such as a government agency, private business, or not-for-profit entity.
Medicaid	Medicaid is the United States health program for families and individuals with low income and resources. It is a means-tested program that is jointly funded by the state and federal governments, and is managed by the states. People served by Medicaid are U.S. citizens or legal permanent residents, including low-income adults, their children, and people with certain disabilities.
Cranial root of accessory nerve	The cranial root of accessory nerve is the smaller of the two portions of the accessory nerve. It is generally considered as a part of the vagus nerve and not part of the accessory nerve proper because the cranial component rapidly joins the vagus nerve and serves the same function as other vagal nerve fibers.
	Its fibers arise from the cells of the nucleus ambiguus and emerge as four or five delicate rootlets from the side of the medulla oblongata, below the roots of the vagus.
Health insurance coverage in the United States	The number of persons without health insurance coverage in the United States is one of the primary concerns raised by advocates of health care reform According to the United States Census Bureau, in 2009 there were 50.7 million people in the US (16.7% of the population) who were without health insurance.
Copayment	In the United States, copayment is accessed. It is technically a form of coinsurance, but is defined differently in health insurance where a coinsurance is a percentage payment after the deductible up to a certain limit. It must be paid before any policy benefit is payable by an insurance company.
Institution	An institution is any structure or mechanism of social order and cooperation governing the behavior of a set of individuals within a given human community. Institutions are identified with a social purpose and permanence, transcending individual human lives and intention by enforcing rules that governs cooperative human behavior.

3. GOVERNMENT AND HEALTH INSURANCE: THE POLICY PROCESS

Policy	A policy is typically described as a principle or rule to guide decisions and achieve rational outcomes. The term is not normally used to denote what is actually done, this is normally referred to as either procedure or protocol. Policies are generally adopted by the Board of or senior governance body within an organization whereas procedures or protocols would be developed and adopted by senior executive officers.
Process	In engineering a process is a set of interrelated tasks that, together, transform inputs into outputs. These tasks may be carried out by people, nature, or machines using resources; so an engineering process must be considered in the context of the agents carrying out the tasks, and the resource attributes involved. Systems Engineering normative documents and those related to Maturity Models are typically based on processes.
Catastrophic	A catastrophe is an extremely large-scale disaster, a horrible event. It may also refer to: · Catastrophe bond, a risk-linked security used to share risks with bond investors · Catastrophe (book), a non-fiction book by Dick Morris and Eileen McGann · Catastrophe (drama), the climax and resolution of a plot in ancient Greek drama and poems · Catastrophe modeling, in Insurance, projecting of the cost of losses due to a catastrophic event · Catastrophe , a 1982 short play by Samuel Beckett · Catastrophe theory, a field of mathematics that studies how the behavior of dynamic systems can change drastically with small variations · Microtubular catastrophe, a feature of the cytoskeleton in eukaryotic cells · Catastrophe (TV series), a five-part science series on Channel 4 a bridge collapses) · catastrophic, a difficulty rating in Dance Dance Revolution · catastrophic, a metal band and side project of Obituary's guitarist Trevor Peres '
Long-term care	Long-term care is a variety of services which help meet both the medical and non-medical needs of people with a chronic illness or disability who cannot care for themselves for long periods of time. It is common for long-term care to provide custodial and non-skilled care, such as assisting with normal daily tasks like dressing, bathing, and using the bathroom. Increasingly, long-term care involves providing a level of medical care that requires the expertise of skilled practitioners to address the often multiple chronic conditions associated with older populations.
Nurse Practitioner	A Nurse Practitioner is an Advanced Practice Nurse (APN) who has completed graduate-level education (either a Master's or a Doctoral degree). Additional APN roles include the Certified Registered Nurse Anesthetist (CRNA)s, CNMs, and CNSs. All Nurse Practitioners are Registered Nurses who have completed extensive additional education, training, and have a dramatically expanded scope of practice over the traditional RN role.

Case study	A case study is an intensive analysis of an individual unit (e.g., a person, group, or event) stressing developmental factors in relation to context. The case study is common in social sciences and life sciences. Case studies may be descriptive or explanatory.

CHAPTER QUIZ: KEY TERMS, PEOPLE, PLACES, CONCEPTS

1. _____ is the unofficial name for Canada's publicly funded universal health insurance system. The formal terminology for the insurance system is provided by the Canada Health Act and the health insurance legislation of the individual provinces and territories.

   Under the terms of the Canada Health Act, all 'insured persons' (basically, legal residents of Canada, including permanent residents) are entitled to receive 'insured services' without copayment.

   a. PAMI
   b. Public health system in India
   c. Medicare
   d. Socialized medicine

2. _____ is a type of financial or other aid provided to people in need and can take many forms in various countries or contexts. In most developed countries, it is largely provided by the government. It may also be organized by charities; informal social groups; religious groups; or inter-governmental organizations such as the United Nations.

   a. 19NorDehydroepiandrosterone
   b. Public health system in India
   c. Welfare
   d. Socialized medicine

3. The number of persons without _____ is one of the primary concerns raised by advocates of health care reform According to the United States Census Bureau, in 2009 there were 50.7 million people in the US (16.7% of the population) who were without health insurance.

   a. Health Security Express
   b. adrenal arteries
   c. Health insurance coverage in the United States
   d. transduction

4. . In economics, a _____ is an intangible commodity. More specifically, _____s are an intangible equivalent of economic goods.

_____ provision is often an economic activity where the buyer does not generally, except by exclusive contract, obtain exclusive ownership of the thing purchased.

a. Shipping list
b. Stockout
c. Service
d. Supply chain

5. A _____ is an intensive analysis of an individual unit (e.g., a person, group, or event) stressing developmental factors in relation to context. The _____ is common in social sciences and life sciences. _____(ies) may be descriptive or explanatory.

a. Clinical study design
b. Construct
c. Case study
d. Cybermethodology

1. c

2. c

3. c

4. c

5. c

You can take the complete Online Interactive Chapter Practice Test

for 3. GOVERNMENT AND HEALTH INSURANCE: THE POLICY PROCESS
on all key terms, persons, places, and concepts.

No Additional Costs

http://www.Cram101.com

Register, send an email request to Travis.Reese@Cram101.com to get your user Id and password.

Include your customer order number, and ISBN number from your studyguide Retailer.

4. COMPARATIVE HEALTH SYSTEMS

CHAPTER OUTLINE: KEY TERMS, PEOPLE, PLACES, CONCEPTS

	Medicare
	Quality assurance
	Health
	Health insurance
	Health system
	Policy
	Accountability
	Health care
	Payroll
	Service
	Intermountain Healthcare
	Hypothetico-deductive model
	Canada Health Act
	Whitehall Study
	Socialized medicine
	Gross domestic product
	Waterlow score
	Barefoot doctor
	Birth
	Primary care
	Projection

	Specialty
	Electronic health record
	Health information technology
	Health record
	Information technology
	RECOrd
	Association
	Safeword
	Health Officers
	Human services
	Life expectancy
	Project
	Case study

4. COMPARATIVE HEALTH SYSTEMS

Medicare	Medicare is the unofficial name for Canada's publicly funded universal health insurance system. The formal terminology for the insurance system is provided by the Canada Health Act and the health insurance legislation of the individual provinces and territories.
	Under the terms of the Canada Health Act, all 'insured persons' (basically, legal residents of Canada, including permanent residents) are entitled to receive 'insured services' without copayment.
Quality assurance	Quality assurance refers to administrative and procedural activities implemented in a quality system so that requirements and goals for a product, service or activity will be fulfilled. It is the systematic measurement, comparison with a standard, monitoring of processes and an associated feedback loop that confers error prevention. This can be contrasted with quality control, which is focused on process outputs.
Health	Health is the level of functional or metabolic efficiency of a living being. In humans, it is the general condition of a person's mind and body, usually meaning to be free from illness, injury or pain (as in 'good health' or 'healthy'). The World Health Organization (WHO) defined health in its broader sense in 1946 as 'a state of complete physical, mental, and social well-being and not merely the absence of disease or infirmity.' Although this definition has been subject to controversy, in particular as lacking operational value and because of the problem created by use of the word 'complete', it remains the most enduring .
Health insurance	Health insurance is insurance against the risk of incurring medical expenses among individuals. By estimating the overall risk of health care and health system expenses among a targeted group, an insurer can develop a routine finance structure, such as a monthly premium or payroll tax, to ensure that money is available to pay for the health care benefits specified in the insurance agreement. The benefit is administered by a central organization such as a government agency, private business, or not-for-profit entity.
Health system	A health system, also sometimes referred to as health care system or healthcare system is the organization of people, institutions, and resources to deliver health care services to meet the health needs of target populations.
	There is a wide variety of health systems around the world, with as many histories and organizational structures as there are nations. In some countries, health system planning is distributed among market participants.
Policy	A policy is typically described as a principle or rule to guide decisions and achieve rational outcomes. The term is not normally used to denote what is actually done, this is normally referred to as either procedure or protocol.

4. COMPARATIVE HEALTH SYSTEMS

Accountability	Accountability is a concept in ethics and governance with several meanings. It is often used synonymously with such concepts as answerability, blameworthiness, liability, and other terms associated with the expectation of account-giving. As an aspect of governance, it has been central to discussions related to problems in the public sector, nonprofit and private (corporate) worlds.
Health care	Health care is the diagnosis, treatment, and prevention of disease, illness, injury, and other physical and mental impairments in humans. Health care is delivered by practitioners in medicine, chiropractic, dentistry, nursing, pharmacy, allied health, and other care providers. It refers to the work done in providing primary care, secondary care and tertiary care, as well as in public health.
Payroll	In a company, payroll is the sum of all financial records of salaries for an employee, wages, bonuses and deductions. In accounting, payroll refers to the amount paid to employees for services they provided during a certain period of time. Payroll plays a major role in a company for several reasons.
Service	In economics, a service is an intangible commodity. More specifically, services are an intangible equivalent of economic goods. Service provision is often an economic activity where the buyer does not generally, except by exclusive contract, obtain exclusive ownership of the thing purchased.
Intermountain Healthcare	Intermountain Health Care, Inc., officially doing business as as Intermountain Healthcare, is a non-profit healthcare system and is the largest healthcare provider in the Intermountain West. Until 2005 it known as Intermountain Health Care or more commonly IHC; it is now. Intermountain Healthcare is headquartered in Salt Lake City, Utah, and currently employs over 32,000 people.
Hypothetico-deductive model	The hypothetico-deductive model, first so-named by William Whewell, is a proposed description of scientific method. According to it, scientific inquiry proceeds by formulating a hypothesis in a form that could conceivably be falsified by a test on observable data. A test that could and does run contrary to predictions of the hypothesis is taken as a falsification of the hypothesis.
Canada Health Act	The Canada Health Act a piece of Canadian federal legislation, adopted in 1984, which specifies the conditions and criteria with which the provincial and territorial health insurance programs must conform in order to receive federal transfer payments under the Canada Health Transfer. These criteria require universal coverage of all insured services (for all 'insured persons') 'Insured health services' means hospital services, physician services and surgical-dental services provided to insured persons, if they are not otherwise covered, for example by Workers Safety Insurance. The Canada Health Act deals only with how the system is financed.

4. COMPARATIVE HEALTH SYSTEMS

Whitehall Study	The original Whitehall Study investigated social determinants of health, specifically the cardiorespiratory disease prevalence and mortality rates among British male civil servants between the ages of 20 and 64. The initial prospective cohort study, the Whitehall I Study, examined over 18,000 male civil servants, and was conducted over a period of ten years, beginning in 1967. A second cohort study, the Whitehall II Study, examined the health of 10,308 civil servants aged 35 to 55, of whom two thirds were men and one third women. The response rate for Whitehall II was 73% in total, 74% for men and 71% for women. A long-term follow-up of study subjects from the first two phases is ongoing.
Socialized medicine	Socialized medicine is a term used in the United States to describe and discuss systems of universal health care - that is, medical and hospital care for all at a nominal cost by means of government regulation of health care and subsidies derived from taxation. Because of historically negative associations with socialism in American culture, the term is usually used pejoratively in American political discourse. The term was first widely used in the United States by advocates of the American Medical Association in opposition to President Harry S. Truman's 1947 health-care initiative.
Gross domestic product	Gross domestic product is the market value of all officially recognized final goods and services produced within a country in a year, or other given period of time. gross domestic product per capita is often considered an indicator of a country's standard of living. gross domestic product per capita is not a measure of personal income .
Waterlow score	The 'Waterlow score gives an estimated risk of a patient developing a pressure sore. It is named after Judy Waterlow.
Barefoot doctor	Barefoot doctors are farmers who received minimal basic medical and paramedical training and worked in rural villages in the People's Republic of China. Their purpose was to bring health care to rural areas where urban-trained doctors would not settle. They promoted basic hygiene, preventive health care, and family planning and treated common illnesses.
Birth	Birth is the act or process of bearing or bringing forth offspring from the uterus. The offspring is brought forth from the mother. The time of human birth is defined as the time at which the fetus comes out of the mother's womb into the world.
Primary care	Primary care is the health care given by a health care provider. Typically this provider acts as the principal point of consultation for patients within a health care system and coordinates other specialists that the patient may need.

4. COMPARATIVE HEALTH SYSTEMS

Projection	Attributing one's own undesirable thoughts, impulses, traits, or behaviors to others is referred to as projection.
Specialty	A specialty in medicine is a branch of medical science. After completing medical school, physicians or surgeons usually further their medical education in a specific specialty of medicine by completing a multiple year residency to become a medical specialist. To a certain extent, medical practitioners have always been specialized.
Electronic health record	An electronic health record is an evolving concept defined as a systematic collection of electronic health information about individual patients or populations. It is a record in digital format that is theoretically capable of being shared across different health care settings. In some cases this sharing can occur by way of network-connected enterprise-wide information systems and other information networks or exchanges.
Health information technology	Health information technology provides the umbrella framework to describe the comprehensive management of health information across computerized systems and its secure exchange between consumers, providers, government and quality entities, and insurers. Health information technology is in general increasingly viewed as the most promising tool for improving the overall quality, safety and efficiency of the health delivery system (Chaudhry et al., 2006). Broad and consistent utilization of Health information technology will:•Improve health care quality;•Prevent medical errors;•Reduce health care costs;•Increase administrative efficiencies;•Decrease paperwork; and•Expand access to affordable care Interoperable Health information technology will improve individual patient care, but it will also bring many public health benefits including:•Early detection of infectious disease outbreaks around the country;•Improved tracking of chronic disease management; and•Evaluation of health care based on value enabled by the collection of de-identified price and quality information that can be compared Concepts and Definitions Health information technology is 'the application of information processing involving both computer hardware and software that deals with the storage, retrieval, sharing, and use of health care information, data, and knowledge for communication and decision making' (Brailer, & Thompson, 2004).
Health record	The terms medical record, health record, and medical chart are used somewhat interchangeably to describe the systematic documentation of a single patient's medical history and care across time within one particular health care provider's jurisdiction. The medical record includes a variety of types of 'notes' entered over time by health care professionals, recording observations and administration of drugs and therapies, orders for the administration of drugs and therapies, test results, x-rays, reports, etc.

Information technology	Information Technology is the branch of engineering that deals with the use of computers and telecommunications to store, retrieve and transmit information.
RECOrd	RECOrd is a Local Biological Records Centre (LRC) serving Cheshire, Halton, Warrington and Wirral (including the vice-county 'pan-handle' boundary around Stockport) - 'The Cheshire region'. It provides a local facility for the storage, validation and usage of Cheshire-based biological data under the National Biodiversity Network (NBN) project. It is one of a number of local Biological Records Centres across Britain which together aim to give complete geographic coverage of the UK. The organisation is housed in Oakfield House at Chester Zoo.
Association	In statistics, an association is any relationship between two measured quantities that renders them statistically dependent. The term 'association' refers broadly to any such relationship, whereas the narrower term 'correlation' refers to a linear relationship between two quantities. There are many statistical measures of association that can be used to infer the presence or absence of an association in a sample of data.
Safeword	A Safeword is a codeword) to unambiguously communicate their physical or emotional state to a dominant (or 'top'), typically when approaching, or crossing, a physical, emotional, or moral boundary. Some Safewords are used to stop the scene outright, while others can communicate a willingness to continue, but at a reduced level of intensity. Safewords are agreed upon before playing a scene by all participants.
Health Officers	Health Officers Health Officers is a common term used in the United States and elsewhere for public health officials. Public health officials may serve at the global, federal, state, county, or municipal level. Health officers are concerned with protecting and improving the health of communities, states, nations and populations.
Human services	Human services refers to a variety of delivery systems such as social welfare services, education, mental health services, and other forms of healthcare. Human services professionals may provide services directly to clients or help clients access services. Human services professionals also manage agencies that provide these services.
Life expectancy	Life expectancy is the expected (in the statistical sense) number of years of life remaining at a given age. It is denoted by e_x, which means the average number of subsequent years of life for someone now aged x, according to a particular mortality experience.

4. COMPARATIVE HEALTH SYSTEMS

Project	A project in business and science is typically defined as a collaborative enterprise, frequently involving research or design, that is carefully planned to achieve a particular aim. Projects can be further defined as temporary rather than permanent social systems that are constituted by teams within or across organizations to accomplish particular tasks under time constraints. Overview The word project comes from the Latin word projectum from the Latin verb proicere, 'before an action' which in turn comes from pro-, which denotes precedence, something that comes before something else in time and iacere, 'to do'.
Case study	A case study is an intensive analysis of an individual unit (e.g., a person, group, or event) stressing developmental factors in relation to context. The case study is common in social sciences and life sciences. Case studies may be descriptive or explanatory.

1. _____ is the level of functional or metabolic efficiency of a living being. In humans, it is the general condition of a person's mind and body, usually meaning to be free from illness, injury or pain (as in 'good _____' or 'healthy'). The World _____ Organization (WHO) defined _____ in its broader sense in 1946 as 'a state of complete physical, mental, and social well-being and not merely the absence of disease or infirmity.' Although this definition has been subject to controversy, in particular as lacking operational value and because of the problem created by use of the word 'complete', it remains the most enduring .

   a. Sano Sansar Initiative
   b. Sex differences in medicine
   c. Health
   d. mortality ratio

2. The '_____ gives an estimated risk of a patient developing a pressure sore. It is named after Judy Waterlow.

   a. 19NorDehydroepiandrosterone
   b. Waterlow score
   c. Medical underwriting
   d. Rohrer's index

3. . In a company, _____ is the sum of all financial records of salaries for an employee, wages, bonuses and deductions. In accounting, _____ refers to the amount paid to employees for services they provided during a certain period of time. _____ plays a major role in a company for several reasons.

a. Payroll

b. NHS primary care trust

c. Primary care physician

d. Primary care

4. _____ is the unofficial name for Canada's publicly funded universal health insurance system. The formal terminology for the insurance system is provided by the Canada Health Act and the health insurance legislation of the individual provinces and territories.

Under the terms of the Canada Health Act, all 'insured persons' (basically, legal residents of Canada, including permanent residents) are entitled to receive 'insured services' without copayment.

a. PAMI

b. Public health system in India

c. Robert Koch Institute

d. Medicare

5. _____ refers to administrative and procedural activities implemented in a quality system so that requirements and goals for a product, service or activity will be fulfilled. It is the systematic measurement, comparison with a standard, monitoring of processes and an associated feedback loop that confers error prevention. This can be contrasted with quality control, which is focused on process outputs.

a. British Accreditation Council

b. Certification

c. Certification and Accreditation

d. Quality assurance

---

1. c
2. b
3. a
4. d
5. d

You can take the complete Online Interactive Chapter Practice Test

for 4. COMPARATIVE HEALTH SYSTEMS
on all key terms, persons, places, and concepts.

No Additional Costs

http://www.Cram101.com

Register, send an email request to Travis.Reese@Cram101.com to get your user Id and password.

Include your customer order number, and ISBN number from your studyguide Retailer.

5. POPULATION HEALTH

CHAPTER OUTLINE: KEY TERMS, PEOPLE, PLACES, CONCEPTS

Health

Ranking

Project

Underinsurance

Medicaid

Health care

Medi-Cal

Medical model

Morbidity

Obesity

Public health

Tobacco

Human services

Service

Whitehall Study

Gradient

Population health

Life expectancy

Health impact assessment

Rate of return

Charity care

	Institution
	Trust
	Wellness
	Transformation
	Accountable care organization
	Initiative
	Case study

Health	Health is the level of functional or metabolic efficiency of a living being. In humans, it is the general condition of a person's mind and body, usually meaning to be free from illness, injury or pain (as in 'good health' or 'healthy'). The World Health Organization (WHO) defined health in its broader sense in 1946 as 'a state of complete physical, mental, and social well-being and not merely the absence of disease or infirmity.' Although this definition has been subject to controversy, in particular as lacking operational value and because of the problem created by use of the word 'complete', it remains the most enduring .
Ranking	A ranking is a relationship between a set of items such that, for any two items, the first is either 'ranked higher than', 'ranked lower than' or 'ranked equal to' the second. In mathematics, this is known as a weak order or total preorder of objects. It is not necessarily a total order of objects because two different objects can have the same ranking.
Project	A project in business and science is typically defined as a collaborative enterprise, frequently involving research or design, that is carefully planned to achieve a particular aim. Projects can be further defined as temporary rather than permanent social systems that are constituted by teams within or across organizations to accomplish particular tasks under time constraints. Overview

5. POPULATION HEALTH

Underinsurance	Condition of average (also called underinsurance in the U.S., or principal of average, subject to average, or pro rata condition of average in Commonwealth countries) is the insurance term used when calculating a payout against a claim where the policy undervalues the sum insured. In the event of partial loss, the amount paid against a claim will be in the same proportion as the value of the underinsurance. The formula used is where Payout is the amount paid out by the policy, Claim is the amount claimed against the policy after a loss, Sum Insured is the maximum amount to be paid out by the policy, and Current Value is the value the policy should be insured for.
Medicaid	Medicaid is the United States health program for families and individuals with low income and resources. It is a means-tested program that is jointly funded by the state and federal governments, and is managed by the states. People served by Medicaid are U.S. citizens or legal permanent residents, including low-income adults, their children, and people with certain disabilities.
Health care	Health care is the diagnosis, treatment, and prevention of disease, illness, injury, and other physical and mental impairments in humans. Health care is delivered by practitioners in medicine, chiropractic, dentistry, nursing, pharmacy, allied health, and other care providers. It refers to the work done in providing primary care, secondary care and tertiary care, as well as in public health.
Medi-Cal	The California Medical Assistance Program (Medi-Cal is the name of the California Medicaid welfare program serving low-income families, seniors, persons with disabilities, children in foster care, pregnant women, and certain low-income adults. It is jointly administered by the California Department of Health Care Services (DHCS) and the Centers for Medicare and Medicaid Services (CMS), with many services implemented at the local level mainly by the counties of California. Approximately 8.8 million citizens were enrolled in Medi-Cal for at least 1 month in 2009-10, or about 23% of California's population.
Medical model	Medical model is the term cited by psychiatrist Ronald D. Laing in his The Politics of the Family and Other Essays (1971), for the 'set of procedures in which all doctors are trained.' This set includes complaint, history, physical examination, ancillary tests if needed, diagnosis, treatment, and prognosis with and without treatment. Sociologist Erving Goffman, in his Asylums, favorably compared the medical model, which was a post-Industrial Revolution occurrence, with the conduct in the tinkering trades (watch, radio, TV repair). The medical model is an approach to pathology that aims to find medical treatments for diagnosed symptoms and syndromes and treats the human body as a very complex mechanism (hence, Goffman's tinkering trade analogy).
Morbidity	Morbidity refers to a diseased state, disability, or poor health due to any cause. The term may be used to refer to the existence of any form of disease, or to the degree that the health condition affects the patient.

Obesity	Obesity is a medical condition in which excess body fat has accumulated to the extent that it may have an adverse effect on health, leading to reduced life expectancy and/or increased health problems. People are considered obese when their body mass index (BMI), a measurement obtained by dividing a person's weight in kilograms by the square of the person's height in metres, exceeds 30 kg/m^2. Obesity increases the likelihood of various diseases, particularly heart disease, type 2 diabetes, obstructive sleep apnea, certain types of cancer, and osteoarthritis.
Public health	Public health is 'the science and art of preventing disease, prolonging life and promoting health through the organized efforts and informed choices of society, organizations, public and private, communities and individuals' (1920, C.E.A. Winslow). It is concerned with threats to health based on population health analysis. The population in question can be as small as a handful of people or as large as all the inhabitants of several continents (for instance, in the case of a pandemic).
Tobacco	Tobacco is an agricultural product processed from the leaves of plants in the genus Nicotiana. It can be consumed, used as a pesticide and, in the form of nicotine tartrate, used in some medicines. It is most commonly used as a drug, and is a valuable cash crop for countries such as Cuba, India, China, and the United States.
Human services	Human services refers to a variety of delivery systems such as social welfare services, education, mental health services, and other forms of healthcare. Human services professionals may provide services directly to clients or help clients access services. Human services professionals also manage agencies that provide these services.
Service	In economics, a service is an intangible commodity. More specifically, services are an intangible equivalent of economic goods. Service provision is often an economic activity where the buyer does not generally, except by exclusive contract, obtain exclusive ownership of the thing purchased.
Whitehall Study	The original Whitehall Study investigated social determinants of health, specifically the cardiorespiratory disease prevalence and mortality rates among British male civil servants between the ages of 20 and 64. The initial prospective cohort study, the Whitehall I Study, examined over 18,000 male civil servants, and was conducted over a period of ten years, beginning in 1967. A second cohort study, the Whitehall II Study, examined the health of 10,308 civil servants aged 35 to 55, of whom two thirds were men and one third women. The response rate for Whitehall II was 73% in total, 74% for men and 71% for women. A long-term follow-up of study subjects from the first two phases is ongoing.
Gradient	In vector calculus, the Gradient of a scalar field is a vector field which points in the direction of the greatest rate of increase of the scalar field, and whose magnitude is the greatest rate of change.

5. POPULATION HEALTH

CHAPTER HIGHLIGHTS & NOTES: KEY TERMS, PEOPLE, PLACES, CONCEPTS

	A generalization of the Gradient for functions on a Euclidean space which have values in another Euclidean space is the Jacobian. A further generalization for a function from one Banach space to another is the Fréchet derivative.
Population health	Population health has been defined as 'the health outcomes of a group of individuals, including the distribution of such outcomes within the group.' It is an approach to health that aims to improve the health of an entire population. One major step in achieving this aim is to reduce health inequities among population groups. Population health seeks to step beyond the individual-level focus of mainstream medicine and public health by addressing a broad range of factors that impact health on a population-level, such as environment, social structure, resource distribution, etc.
Life expectancy	Life expectancy is the expected (in the statistical sense) number of years of life remaining at a given age. It is denoted by e_x, which means the average number of subsequent years of life for someone now aged x, according to a particular mortality experience. (In technical literature, this symbol means the average number of complete years of life remaining, excluding fractions of a year.
Health impact assessment	Health Impact Assessment is defined as 'a combination of procedures, methods and tools by which a policy, program or project may be judged as to its potential effects on the health of a population, and the distribution of those effects within the population.' (ECHP 1999, p. 4) HIA is intended to produce a set of evidence-based recommendations to inform decision-making (Taylor & Quigley 2002, p. 2). HIA seeks to maximise the positive health impacts and minimise the negative health impacts of proposed policies, programs or projects. The procedures of HIA are similar to those used in other forms of impact assessment, such as environmental impact assessment or social impact assessment.
Rate of return	In finance, rate of return also known as return on investment (ROI), rate of profit or sometimes just return, is the ratio of money gained or lost (whether realized or unrealized) on an investment relative to the amount of money invested. The amount of money gained or lost may be referred to as interest, profit/loss, gain/loss, or net income/loss. The money invested may be referred to as the asset, capital, principal, or the cost basis of the investment.
Charity care	In the United States, charity care is health care provided for free or at reduced prices to low income patients. The percentage of doctors providing charity care dropped from 76% in 1996-97 to 68% in 2004-2005. Potential reasons for the decline include changes in physician practice patterns and increasing financial pressures. In 2006, Senate investigators found that many hospitals did not inform patients that charity care was available.

5. POPULATION HEALTH

Institution	An institution is any structure or mechanism of social order and cooperation governing the behavior of a set of individuals within a given human community. Institutions are identified with a social purpose and permanence, transcending individual human lives and intention by enforcing rules that governs cooperative human behavior. The term 'institution' is commonly applied to customs and behavior patterns important to a society, as well as to particular formal organizations of government and public service.
Trust	In a social context, trust has several connotations. Definitions of trust typically refer to a situation characterised by the following aspects: One party (trustor) is willing to rely on the actions of another party (trustee); the situation is directed to the future. In addition, the trustor (voluntarily or forcedly) abandons control over the actions performed by the trustee.
Wellness	Wellness is generally used to mean a healthy balance of the mind, body and spirit that results in an overall feeling of well-being. It has been used in the context of alternative medicine since Halbert L. Dunn, M.D., began using the phrase high level wellness in the 1950s. The modern concept of wellness did not, however, become popular until the 1970s.
Transformation	· transformation · transformation · Data transformation · Phase transformation, a physical transition from one medium to another · Chemical transformation · Metamorphosis, the biological process of changing physical form after birth or hatching · Malignant transformation, the process of cells becoming cancerous · transformation genetic alteration of a cell by DNA uptake · Data transformation · Model transformation · Program transformation · XML transformation · transformation of text · transformation by Carol Berg · Shapeshifting, a type of transformation common in mythology and folklore · Henshin, a type of transformation common in anime, manga and tokusatsu · transformation a concept in copyright law · transformation · transformation · transformation · transformation of culture · transformation design, a design process · transformation fetish · transformation playing card · transformation problem, a concept in economics · transformational grammar · Spiritual transformation · Business Network transformation .
Accountable care organization	An accountable care organization is a healthcare organization characterized by a payment and care delivery model that seeks to tie provider reimbursements to quality metrics and reductions in the total cost of care for an assigned population of patients. A group of coordinated health care providers forms an Accountable care organization, which then provides care to a group of patients.

5. POPULATION HEALTH

Initiative	An initiative represents an enterprise's readiness to embark on a new venture. Generally speaking, the motivation for an initiative arises from a desire to accomplish something that would benefit the enterprise, such as improving productivity, reducing costs or increasing market share.
	A typical initiative is expressed as a process and includes metrics and time frames.
Case study	A case study is an intensive analysis of an individual unit (e.g., a person, group, or event) stressing developmental factors in relation to context. The case study is common in social sciences and life sciences. Case studies may be descriptive or explanatory.

1. _____ is an agricultural product processed from the leaves of plants in the genus Nicotiana. It can be consumed, used as a pesticide and, in the form of nicotine tartrate, used in some medicines. It is most commonly used as a drug, and is a valuable cash crop for countries such as Cuba, India, China, and the United States.

   a. Yerba mate
   b. 19NorDehydroepiandrosterone
   c. 2 mile
   d. Tobacco

2. In a social context, _____ has several connotations. Definitions of _____ typically refer to a situation characterised by the following aspects: One party (trustor) is willing to rely on the actions of another party (trustee); the situation is directed to the future. In addition, the trustor (voluntarily or forcedly) abandons control over the actions performed by the trustee.

   a. Trust
   b. International Psychoanalytical Association
   c. Emil Kraepelin
   d. Arnold Pick

3. . _____ is the level of functional or metabolic efficiency of a living being. In humans, it is the general condition of a person's mind and body, usually meaning to be free from illness, injury or pain (as in 'good _____' or 'healthy'). The World _____ Organization (WHO) defined _____ in its broader sense in 1946 as 'a state of complete physical, mental, and social well-being and not merely the absence of disease or infirmity.' Although this definition has been subject to controversy, in particular as lacking operational value and because of the problem created by use of the word 'complete', it remains the most enduring .

   a. Sano Sansar Initiative

b. Health

c. Sleep Cycle Alarm Clock

d. mortality ratio

4. _____ refers to a diseased state, disability, or poor health due to any cause. The term may be used to refer to the existence of any form of disease, or to the degree that the health condition affects the patient. Among severely ill patients, the level of _____ is often measured by ICU scoring systems.

a. Papilloma

b. Monostotic fibrous dysplasia

c. 19NorDehydroepiandrosterone

d. Morbidity

5. A _____ is a relationship between a set of items such that, for any two items, the first is either 'ranked higher than', 'ranked lower than' or 'ranked equal to' the second. In mathematics, this is known as a weak order or total preorder of objects. It is not necessarily a total order of objects because two different objects can have the same _____.

a. Ranking

b. Resampling

c. Semiparametric regression

d. Sign test

1. d
2. a
3. b
4. d
5. a

You can take the complete Online Interactive Chapter Practice Test

for 5. POPULATION HEALTH
on all key terms, persons, places, and concepts.

No Additional Costs

http://www.Cram101.com

Register, send an email request to Travis.Reese@Cram101.com to get your user Id and password.

Include your customer order number, and ISBN number from your studyguide Retailer.

6. PUBLIC HEALTH: A TRANSFORMATION FOR THE 21ST CENTURY

_____ Consolidated Omnibus Budget Reconciliation Act

_____ Medi-Cal

_____ Closures

_____ Adrenal gland disorders

_____ Disease prevention

_____ Health

_____ Health promotion

_____ Promotion

_____ Department of Health and Human Services

_____ Income

_____ Medicare

_____ Service

_____ Policy

_____ Public health

_____ Accreditation

_____ Association

_____ Health department

_____ Environmental enrichment

_____ Environmental protection

_____ Local health department

_____ Infrastructure

CHAPTER OUTLINE: KEY TERMS, PEOPLE, PLACES, CONCEPTS

	Effective
	Health impact assessment
	Resource
	Case study

CHAPTER HIGHLIGHTS & NOTES: KEY TERMS, PEOPLE, PLACES, CONCEPTS

Consolidated Omnibus Budget Reconciliation Act	The Consolidated Omnibus Budget Reconciliation Act of 1985, is a law passed by the U.S. Congress and signed by President Reagan that, among other things, mandates an insurance program giving some employees the ability to continue health insurance coverage after leaving employment. Consolidated Omnibus Budget Reconciliation Act includes amendments to the Employee Retirement Income Security Act of 1974 (ERISA). The law deals with a great variety of subjects, such as tobacco price supports, railroads, private pension plans, disability insurance, and the postal service , but it is perhaps best known for Title X, which amends the Internal Revenue Code and the Public Health Service Act to deny income tax deductions to employers for contributions to a group health plan unless such plan meets certain continuing coverage requirements.
Medi-Cal	The California Medical Assistance Program (Medi-Cal is the name of the California Medicaid welfare program serving low-income families, seniors, persons with disabilities, children in foster care, pregnant women, and certain low-income adults. It is jointly administered by the California Department of Health Care Services (DHCS) and the Centers for Medicare and Medicaid Services (CMS), with many services implemented at the local level mainly by the counties of California. Approximately 8.8 million citizens were enrolled in Medi-Cal for at least 1 month in 2009-10, or about 23% of California's population.
Closures	Closures are devices and techniques used to close a bottle, jug, jar, can, which is the process of treating and handling food to stop or greatly slow down spoilage (loss of quality, edibility or nutritive value) caused or accelerated by micro-organisms. Closures make it possible to preserve food and beverages for a long period of time by reducing the food/beverage's exposure to microorganisms.
Adrenal gland disorders	Adrenal gland disorders (or diseases) are conditions that interfere with the normal functioning of the adrenal glands. They are characterized by adrenal insufficiencies, where there are deficiencies in the availability of steroids that are produced by the adrenal glands.

6. PUBLIC HEALTH: A TRANSFORMATION FOR THE 21ST CENTURY

Disease prevention	Preventive healthcare consists of measures taken for disease prevention, as opposed to disease treatment. Just as health encompasses a variety of physical and mental states, so do disease and disability, which are affected by environmental factors, genetic predisposition, disease agents, and lifestyle choices. Health, disease, and disability are dynamic processes which begin before individuals realize they are affected.
Health	Health is the level of functional or metabolic efficiency of a living being. In humans, it is the general condition of a person's mind and body, usually meaning to be free from illness, injury or pain (as in 'good health' or 'healthy'). The World Health Organization (WHO) defined health in its broader sense in 1946 as 'a state of complete physical, mental, and social well-being and not merely the absence of disease or infirmity.' Although this definition has been subject to controversy, in particular as lacking operational value and because of the problem created by use of the word 'complete', it remains the most enduring .
Health promotion	Health promotion has been defined by the World Health Organization's 2005 Bangkok Charter for Health Promotion in a Globalized World as 'the process of enabling people to increase control over their health and its determinants, and thereby improve their health'. The primary means of health promotion occur through developing healthy public policy that addresses the prerequisites of health such as income, housing, food security, employment, and quality working conditions. There is a tendency among public health officials and governments--and this is especially the case in liberal nations such as Canada and the USA--to reduce health promotion to health education and social marketing focused on changing behavioral risk factors.
Promotion	A promotion is the advancement of an employee's rank or position in an organizational hierarchy system. Promotion may be an employee's reward for good performance, i.e., positive appraisal. Before a company promotes an employee to a particular position it ensures that the person is able to handle the added responsibilities by screening the employee with interviews and tests and giving them training or on-the-job experience.
Department of Health and Human Services	The United States Department of Health and Human Services (HHS) is a Cabinet department of the United States government with the goal of protecting the health of all Americans and providing essential human services. Its motto is 'Improving the health, safety, and well-being of America'. Before its education functions were spun off in 1979, it was called the Department of Health, Education, and Welfare. · 1 History · 2 Agencies · 2.1 Office of the Secretary (OS) · 2.2 Operating divisions · 3 · Immediate Office of the Secretary (IOS) - currently led by Kathleen Sebelius · Office of the Deputy Secretary (DS) - currently led by Deputy Secretary Bill Corr · Assistant Secretary for Administration and Management (ASAM)

· Program Support Center (PSC) - currently led by Director Philip Van Landingham · Assistant Secretary for Legislation (ASL) · Assistant Secretary for Planning and Evaluation (ASPE) · Assistant Secretary for Preparedness and Response (ASPR)

· Biomedical Advanced Research and Development Authority (BARDA)

· Project BioShield · Public Health Emergency Medical Countermeasures Enterprise (PHEMCE) · Assistant Secretary for Public Affairs (ASPA) · Assistant Secretary for Resources and Technology (ASRT) · Departmental Appeals Board (DAB) · Office for Civil Rights (OCR) · Office of Global Health Affairs (OGHA) · Office of Intergovernmental Affairs (IGA) · Office of the Secretary's Regional Directors · Office of the General Counsel (OGC) · Office of Inspector General (OIG) - currently led by Inspector General Daniel R. Levinson · Office of Medicare Hearings and Appeals (OMHA) · Office of the National Coordinator for Health Information Technology (ONC) · Public Health Service (PHS) / Office of the Assistant Secretary for Health (ASH) - currently led by Assistant Secretary, Howard K. Koh

· Office of Public Health and Science (OPHS) · Office of the Surgeon General - currently led by Acting Surgeon General, Rear Admiral Steven K. Galson

· U.S. Public Health Service (USPHS) Commissioned Corps · Office on Disability (OD - currently led by Director Henry Claypool · Center for Faith-Based and Community Initiatives (CFBCI)

· Administration for Children and Families (ACF) - currently led by Principal Deputy Assistant Secretary David Hansell · Administration on Aging (AoA) - currently led by Assistant Secretary Kathy Greenlee · Agency for Healthcare Research and Quality (AHRQ) - currently led by Director Carolyn Clancy · Agency for Toxic Substances and Disease Registry (ATSDR) - currently led by Administrator Thomas R. Frieden · Centers for Disease Control and Prevention (CDC) - currently led by Director Thomas R. Frieden · Centers for Medicare and Medicaid Services (CMS)- currently led by Acting Administrator Charlene Frizzera · Food and Drug Administration (FDA) - currently led by Commissioner Margaret Hamburg · Health Resources and Services Administration (HRSA) - currently led by Administrator Mary Wakefield · Indian Health Service (IHS) - currently led by Acting Director, Robert G. McSwain · National Institutes of Health (NIH) - currently led by Director Francis Collins · Substance Abuse and Mental Health Services Administration (SAMHSA) - currently led by Administrator Charles Curie

(Several agencies within HHS are components of the Public Health Service (PHS), including AHRQ, ASPR, ATSDR, CDC, FDA, HRSA, IHS, NIH, SAMHSA, OGHA, and OPHS).

· Social Security Administration, made independent in 1995. · Health Care Financing Administration

The Department of Health and Human Services' budget includes more than 300 programs, covering a wide spectrum of activities. Some highlights include:

· Health and social science research · Preventing disease, including immunization services · Assuring food and drug safety · Medicare (health insurance for elderly and disabled Americans) and Medicaid (health insurance for low-income people) · Health information technology · Financial assistance and services for low-income families · Improving maternal and infant health, including a Nurse Home Visitation to support first-time mothers. · Head Start (pre-school education and services) · Faith-based and community initiatives · Preventing child abuse and domestic violence · Substance abuse treatment and prevention · Services for older Americans, including home-delivered meals · Comprehensive health services for Native Americans · Medical preparedness for emergencies, including potential terrorism.

Income	Income is the consumption and savings opportunity gained by an entity within a specified timeframe, which is generally expressed in monetary terms. However, for households and individuals, 'income is the sum of all the wages, salaries, profits, interests payments, rents and other forms of earnings received... in a given period of time.' In the field of public economics, the term may refer to the accumulation of both monetary and non-monetary consumption ability, with the former (monetary) being used as a proxy for total income. Increase in income Income per capita has been increasing steadily in almost every country.
Medicare	Medicare is the unofficial name for Canada's publicly funded universal health insurance system. The formal terminology for the insurance system is provided by the Canada Health Act and the health insurance legislation of the individual provinces and territories. Under the terms of the Canada Health Act, all 'insured persons' (basically, legal residents of Canada, including permanent residents) are entitled to receive 'insured services' without copayment.
Service	In economics, a service is an intangible commodity. More specifically, services are an intangible equivalent of economic goods. Service provision is often an economic activity where the buyer does not generally, except by exclusive contract, obtain exclusive ownership of the thing purchased.
Policy	A policy is typically described as a principle or rule to guide decisions and achieve rational outcomes. The term is not normally used to denote what is actually done, this is normally referred to as either procedure or protocol.

Public health	Public health is 'the science and art of preventing disease, prolonging life and promoting health through the organized efforts and informed choices of society, organizations, public and private, communities and individuals' (1920, C.E.A. Winslow). It is concerned with threats to health based on population health analysis. The population in question can be as small as a handful of people or as large as all the inhabitants of several continents (for instance, in the case of a pandemic).
Accreditation	Accreditation is a process in which certification of competency, authority, or credibility is presented. Organizations that issue credentials or certify third parties against official standards are themselves formally accredited by accreditation bodies (such as UKAS); hence they are sometimes known as 'accredited certification bodies'. The accreditation process ensures that their certification practices are acceptable, typically meaning that they are competent to test and certify third parties, behave ethically and employ suitable quality assurance.
Association	In statistics, an association is any relationship between two measured quantities that renders them statistically dependent. The term 'association' refers broadly to any such relationship, whereas the narrower term 'correlation' refers to a linear relationship between two quantities. There are many statistical measures of association that can be used to infer the presence or absence of an association in a sample of data.
Health department	A health department is a part of government which focuses on issues related to the general health of the citizenry. Subnational entities, such as states, counties and cities, often also operate a health department of their own. Health departments perform food licensing and food inspection (the person who performs this job is often called a Health Inspector), vaccination programs, free STD and HIV tests, and other medical assistance.
Environmental enrichment	Environmental enrichment concerns how the brain is affected by the stimulation of its information processing provided by its surroundings (including the opportunity to interact socially). Brains in richer, more stimulating environments, have increased numbers of synapses, and the dendrite arbors upon which they reside are more complex. This effect happens particularly during neurodevelopment, but also to a lesser degree in adulthood.
Environmental protection	Environmental protection is a practice of protecting the natural environment on individual, organizational or governmental levels, for the benefit of the natural environment and humans. Due to the pressures of population and technology, the biophysical environment is being degraded, sometimes permanently. This has been recognized, and governments have begun placing restraints on activities that cause environmental degradation.
Local health department	A local health department is a government agency on the front lines of public health. Local health departments may be entities of local or state government and often report to a mayor, city council, county board of health or county commission.

6. PUBLIC HEALTH: A TRANSFORMATION FOR THE 21ST CENTURY

Infrastructure	Infrastructure is basic physical and organizational structures needed for the operation of a society or enterprise, or the services and facilities necessary for an economy to function. It can be generally defined as the set of interconnected structural elements that provide framework supporting an entire structure of development. It is an important term for judging a country or region's development.
Effective	Effective is a database of predicted bacterial secreted proteins.
Health impact assessment	Health Impact Assessment is defined as 'a combination of procedures, methods and tools by which a policy, program or project may be judged as to its potential effects on the health of a population, and the distribution of those effects within the population.' (ECHP 1999, p. 4) HIA is intended to produce a set of evidence-based recommendations to inform decision-making (Taylor & Quigley 2002, p. 2). HIA seeks to maximise the positive health impacts and minimise the negative health impacts of proposed policies, programs or projects. The procedures of HIA are similar to those used in other forms of impact assessment, such as environmental impact assessment or social impact assessment.
Resource	In project management terminology, resources are required to carry out the project tasks. They can be people, equipment, facilities, funding, or anything else capable of definition (usually other than labour) required for the completion of a project activity. The lack of a resource will therefore be a constraint on the completion of the project activity.
Case study	A case study is an intensive analysis of an individual unit (e.g., a person, group, or event) stressing developmental factors in relation to context. The case study is common in social sciences and life sciences. Case studies may be descriptive or explanatory.

1. The California Medical Assistance Program (_____ is the name of the California Medicaid welfare program serving low-income families, seniors, persons with disabilities, children in foster care, pregnant women, and certain low-income adults. It is jointly administered by the California Department of Health Care Services (DHCS) and the Centers for Medicare and Medicaid Services (CMS), with many services implemented at the local level mainly by the counties of California. Approximately 8.8 million citizens were enrolled in _____ for at least 1 month in 2009-10, or about 23% of California's population.

   a. Medical billing
   b. Medi-Cal
   c. Medicare Advantage
   d. Medicare and Medicaid Extenders Act of 2010

2. . The United States _____ (HHS) is a Cabinet department of the United States government with the goal of protecting the health of all Americans and providing essential human services. Its motto is 'Improving the health, safety, and well-being of America'. Before its education functions were spun off in 1979, it was called the Department of Health, Education, and Welfare.

   · 1 History · 2 Agencies

   · 2.1 Office of the Secretary (OS) · 2.2 Operating divisions · 3

   · Immediate Office of the Secretary (IOS) - currently led by Kathleen Sebelius · Office of the Deputy Secretary (DS) - currently led by Deputy Secretary Bill Corr · Assistant Secretary for Administration and Management (ASAM)

   · Program Support Center (PSC) - currently led by Director Philip Van Landingham · Assistant Secretary for Legislation (ASL) · Assistant Secretary for Planning and Evaluation (ASPE) · Assistant Secretary for Preparedness and Response (ASPR)

   · Biomedical Advanced Research and Development Authority (BARDA)

   · Project BioShield · Public Health Emergency Medical Countermeasures Enterprise (PHEMCE) · Assistant Secretary for Public Affairs (ASPA) · Assistant Secretary for Resources and Technology (ASRT) · Departmental Appeals Board (DAB) · Office for Civil Rights (OCR) · Office of Global Health Affairs (OGHA) · Office of Intergovernmental Affairs (IGA) · Office of the Secretary's Regional Directors · Office of the General Counsel (OGC) · Office of Inspector General (OIG) - currently led by Inspector General Daniel R. Levinson · Office of Medicare Hearings and Appeals (OMHA) · Office of the National Coordinator for Health Information Technology (ONC) · Public Health Service (PHS) / Office of the Assistant Secretary for Health (ASH) - currently led by Assistant Secretary, Howard K. Koh

   · Office of Public Health and Science (OPHS) · Office of the Surgeon General - currently led by Acting Surgeon General, Rear Admiral Steven K. Galson

   · U.S. Public Health Service (USPHS) Commissioned Corps · Office on Disability (OD - currently led by Director Henry Claypool · Center for Faith-Based and Community Initiatives (CFBCI)

· Administration for Children and Families (ACF) - currently led by Principal Deputy Assistant Secretary David Hansell · Administration on Aging (AoA) - currently led by Assistant Secretary Kathy Greenlee · Agency for Healthcare Research and Quality (AHRQ) - currently led by Director Carolyn Clancy · Agency for Toxic Substances and Disease Registry (ATSDR) - currently led by Administrator Thomas R. Frieden · Centers for Disease Control and Prevention (CDC) - currently led by Director Thomas R. Frieden · Centers for Medicare and Medicaid Services (CMS)- currently led by Acting Administrator Charlene Frizzera · Food and Drug Administration (FDA) - currently led by Commissioner Margaret Hamburg · Health Resources and Services Administration (HRSA) - currently led by Administrator Mary Wakefield · Indian Health Service (IHS) - currently led by Acting Director, Robert G. McSwain · National Institutes of Health (NIH) - currently led by Director Francis Collins · Substance Abuse and Mental Health Services Administration (SAMHSA) - currently led by Administrator Charles Curie

(Several agencies within HHS are components of the Public Health Service (PHS), including AHRQ, ASPR, ATSDR, CDC, FDA, HRSA, IHS, NIH, SAMHSA, OGHA, and OPHS).

· Social Security Administration, made independent in 1995. · Health Care Financing Administration

The _____' budget includes more than 300 programs, covering a wide spectrum of activities. Some highlights include:

· Health and social science research · Preventing disease, including immunization services · Assuring food and drug safety · Medicare (health insurance for elderly and disabled Americans) and Medicaid (health insurance for low-income people) · Health information technology · Financial assistance and services for low-income families · Improving maternal and infant health, including a Nurse Home Visitation to support first-time mothers. · Head Start (pre-school education and services) · Faith-based and community initiatives · Preventing child abuse and domestic violence · Substance abuse treatment and prevention · Services for older Americans, including home-delivered meals · Comprehensive health services for Native Americans · Medical preparedness for emergencies, including potential terrorism.

a. Physical Activity Guidelines for Americans
b. Department of Health and Human Services
c. National Advisory Committee on Microbiological Criteria for Foods
d. Public Health Emergency Preparedness

3. . _____ has been defined by the World Health Organization's 2005 Bangkok Charter for _____ in a Globalized World as 'the process of enabling people to increase control over their health and its determinants, and thereby improve their health'. The primary means of _____ occur through developing healthy public policy that addresses the prerequisites of health such as income, housing, food security, employment, and quality working conditions. There is a tendency among public health officials and governments--and this is especially the case in liberal nations such as Canada and the USA--to reduce _____ to health education and social marketing focused on changing behavioral risk factors.

a. Health Sciences Online
b. Health promotion
c. Maria Deloria Knoll

4. The _____ of 1985, is a law passed by the U.S. Congress and signed by President Reagan that, among other things, mandates an insurance program giving some employees the ability to continue health insurance coverage after leaving employment. _____ includes amendments to the Employee Retirement Income Security Act of 1974 (ERISA). The law deals with a great variety of subjects, such as tobacco price supports, railroads, private pension plans, disability insurance, and the postal service , but it is perhaps best known for Title X, which amends the Internal Revenue Code and the Public Health Service Act to deny income tax deductions to employers for contributions to a group health plan unless such plan meets certain continuing coverage requirements.

    a. 19NorDehydroepiandrosterone
    b. Consolidated Omnibus Budget Reconciliation Act
    c. 21-Hydroxylase
    d. 3-MCPD

5. Preventive healthcare consists of measures taken for _____, as opposed to disease treatment. Just as health encompasses a variety of physical and mental states, so do disease and disability, which are affected by environmental factors, genetic predisposition, disease agents, and lifestyle choices. Health, disease, and disability are dynamic processes which begin before individuals realize they are affected.

    a. 19NorDehydroepiandrosterone
    b. Disease prevention
    c. Apparent mineralocorticoid excess
    d. Aseptic meningitis

1. b
2. b
3. b
4. b
5. b

You can take the complete Online Interactive Chapter Practice Test

for 6. PUBLIC HEALTH: A TRANSFORMATION FOR THE 21ST CENTURY
on all key terms, persons, places, and concepts.

No Additional Costs

http://www.Cram101.com

Register, send an email request to Travis.Reese@Cram101.com to get your user Id and password.

Include your customer order number, and ISBN number from your studyguide Retailer.

7. HEALTH AND BEHAVIOR

CHAPTER OUTLINE: KEY TERMS, PEOPLE, PLACES, CONCEPTS

Tobacco

Alcohol

Health

Sedentary lifestyle

Obesity

Theories

Whitehall Study

Social learning theory

Department of Health and Human Services

Service

Marketing

Social marketing

Public health

Intervention

Primary care

Institution

Social ecological model

Policy

Control

Childhood obesity

Consolidated Omnibus Budget Reconciliation Act

CHAPTER OUTLINE: KEY TERMS, PEOPLE, PLACES, CONCEPTS

	Safeword
	Crossing the Quality Chasm
	Chronic
	Chronic care
	Health care
	Medi-Cal
	Medical home
	Copayment
	Paradigm
	Quality improvement
	Trial
	Initiative
	Case study

7. HEALTH AND BEHAVIOR

Tobacco	Tobacco is an agricultural product processed from the leaves of plants in the genus Nicotiana. It can be consumed, used as a pesticide and, in the form of nicotine tartrate, used in some medicines. It is most commonly used as a drug, and is a valuable cash crop for countries such as Cuba, India, China, and the United States.
Alcohol	In chemistry, an alcohol is an organic compound in which the hydroxyl functional group is bound to a carbon atom. In particular, this carbon center should be saturated, having single bonds to three other atoms. An important class of alcohols are the simple acyclic alcohols, the general formula for which is $CH_{2n+1}OH$. Of those, ethanol (CÃƒÆ'Ã†â€™ÃƒÂ¢â€šÂ¬Ã¢â€žÂ¢ÃƒÂ¢â€šÂ¬Ã¢â€šÂ¬...ÃƒÆ'Ã†â€™ÃƒÂ¢â€šÂ¬Ã‚Â¢ÃƒÆ'Ã¢â‚¬ÂÃƒÂ¢â€šÂ¬ÃƒÂ¢â€šÂ¬Ã‚Â¢ÃƒÆ'Ã†â€™ÃƒÂ¢â€šÂ¬Ã…Â¡ÃƒÂ¢â€šÂ¬Ã‚Â¬...ÃƒÆ'Ã†â€™ÃƒÂ¢â€šÂ¬Ã¢â€žÂ¢ÃƒÂ¢â€šÂ¬Ã…Â¡Ã¢â‚¬Â¢ÃƒÆ'Ã¢â‚¬ÂÃ†â€™â€¦OH) is the type of alcohol found in alcoholic beverages, and in common speech the word alcohol refers specifically to ethanol.
Health	Health is the level of functional or metabolic efficiency of a living being. In humans, it is the general condition of a person's mind and body, usually meaning to be free from illness, injury or pain (as in 'good health' or 'healthy'). The World Health Organization (WHO) defined health in its broader sense in 1946 as 'a state of complete physical, mental, and social well-being and not merely the absence of disease or infirmity.' Although this definition has been subject to controversy, in particular as lacking operational value and because of the problem created by use of the word 'complete', it remains the most enduring .
Sedentary lifestyle	A sedentary lifestyle is a type of lifestyle with no or irregular physical activity. A person who lives a sedentary lifestyle may colloquially be known as a couch potato. It is commonly found in both the developed and developing world.
Obesity	Obesity is a medical condition in which excess body fat has accumulated to the extent that it may have an adverse effect on health, leading to reduced life expectancy and/or increased health problems. People are considered obese when their body mass index (BMI), a measurement obtained by dividing a person's weight in kilograms by the square of the person's height in metres, exceeds 30 kg/m^2.

7. HEALTH AND BEHAVIOR

Theories	[For a more detailed account of theories as expressed in formal language as they are studied in mathematical logic see Theory (mathematical logic.)] The term theory has two broad sets of meanings, one used in the empirical sciences (both natural and social) and the other used in philosophy, mathematics, logic, and across other fields in the humanities. There is considerable difference and even dispute across academic disciplines as to the proper usages of the term. What follows is an attempt to describe how the term is used, not to try to say how it ought to be used.
Whitehall Study	The original Whitehall Study investigated social determinants of health, specifically the cardiorespiratory disease prevalence and mortality rates among British male civil servants between the ages of 20 and 64. The initial prospective cohort study, the Whitehall I Study, examined over 18,000 male civil servants, and was conducted over a period of ten years, beginning in 1967. A second cohort study, the Whitehall II Study, examined the health of 10,308 civil servants aged 35 to 55, of whom two thirds were men and one third women. The response rate for Whitehall II was 73% in total, 74% for men and 71% for women. A long-term follow-up of study subjects from the first two phases is ongoing.
Social learning theory	Social learning theory is a perspective that states that people learn within a social context. It is facilitated through concepts such as modeling and observational learning. People, especially children, learn from the environment and seek acceptance from society by learning through influential models.
Department of Health and Human Services	The United States Department of Health and Human Services (HHS) is a Cabinet department of the United States government with the goal of protecting the health of all Americans and providing essential human services. Its motto is 'Improving the health, safety, and well-being of America'. Before its education functions were spun off in 1979, it was called the Department of Health, Education, and Welfare. · 1 History · 2 Agencies · 2.1 Office of the Secretary (OS) · 2.2 Operating divisions · 3 · Immediate Office of the Secretary (IOS) - currently led by Kathleen Sebelius · Office of the Deputy Secretary (DS) - currently led by Deputy Secretary Bill Corr · Assistant Secretary for Administration and Management (ASAM) · Program Support Center (PSC) - currently led by Director Philip Van Landingham · Assistant Secretary for Legislation (ASL) · Assistant Secretary for Planning and Evaluation (ASPE) · Assistant Secretary for Preparedness and Response (ASPR) · Biomedical Advanced Research and Development Authority (BARDA)

7. HEALTH AND BEHAVIOR

· Project BioShield · Public Health Emergency Medical Countermeasures Enterprise (PHEMCE) · Assistant Secretary for Public Affairs (ASPA) · Assistant Secretary for Resources and Technology (ASRT) · Departmental Appeals Board (DAB) · Office for Civil Rights (OCR) · Office of Global Health Affairs (OGHA) · Office of Intergovernmental Affairs (IGA) · Office of the Secretary's Regional Directors · Office of the General Counsel (OGC) · Office of Inspector General (OIG) - currently led by Inspector General Daniel R. Levinson · Office of Medicare Hearings and Appeals (OMHA) · Office of the National Coordinator for Health Information Technology (ONC) · Public Health Service (PHS) / Office of the Assistant Secretary for Health (ASH) - currently led by Assistant Secretary, Howard K. Koh

· Office of Public Health and Science (OPHS) · Office of the Surgeon General - currently led by Acting Surgeon General, Rear Admiral Steven K. Galson

· U.S. Public Health Service (USPHS) Commissioned Corps · Office on Disability (OD - currently led by Director Henry Claypool · Center for Faith-Based and Community Initiatives (CFBCI)

· Administration for Children and Families (ACF) - currently led by Principal Deputy Assistant Secretary David Hansell · Administration on Aging (AoA) - currently led by Assistant Secretary Kathy Greenlee · Agency for Healthcare Research and Quality (AHRQ) - currently led by Director Carolyn Clancy · Agency for Toxic Substances and Disease Registry (ATSDR) - currently led by Administrator Thomas R. Frieden · Centers for Disease Control and Prevention (CDC) - currently led by Director Thomas R. Frieden · Centers for Medicare and Medicaid Services (CMS)- currently led by Acting Administrator Charlene Frizzera · Food and Drug Administration (FDA) - currently led by Commissioner Margaret Hamburg · Health Resources and Services Administration (HRSA) - currently led by Administrator Mary Wakefield · Indian Health Service (IHS) - currently led by Acting Director, Robert G. McSwain · National Institutes of Health (NIH) - currently led by Director Francis Collins · Substance Abuse and Mental Health Services Administration (SAMHSA) - currently led by Administrator Charles Curie

(Several agencies within HHS are components of the Public Health Service (PHS), including AHRQ, ASPR, ATSDR, CDC, FDA, HRSA, IHS, NIH, SAMHSA, OGHA, and OPHS).

· Social Security Administration, made independent in 1995. · Health Care Financing Administration

The Department of Health and Human Services' budget includes more than 300 programs, covering a wide spectrum of activities. Some highlights include:

· Health and social science research · Preventing disease, including immunization services · Assuring food and drug safety · Medicare (health insurance for elderly and disabled Americans) and Medicaid (health insurance for low-income people) · Health information technology · Financial assistance and services for low-income families

	· Improving maternal and infant health, including a Nurse Home Visitation to support first-time mothers. · Head Start (pre-school education and services) · Faith-based and community initiatives · Preventing child abuse and domestic violence · Substance abuse treatment and prevention · Services for older Americans, including home-delivered meals · Comprehensive health services for Native Americans · Medical preparedness for emergencies, including potential terrorism.
Service	In economics, a service is an intangible commodity. More specifically, services are an intangible equivalent of economic goods. Service provision is often an economic activity where the buyer does not generally, except by exclusive contract, obtain exclusive ownership of the thing purchased.
Marketing	Marketing is a 'social and managerial process by which individuals and groups obtain what they need and want through creating and exchanging products and values with others.' It is an integrated process through which companies create value for customers and build strong customer relationships in order to capture value from customers in return. Marketing is used to create the customer, to keep the customer and to satisfy the customer. With the customer as the focus of its activities, it can be concluded that Marketing management is one of the major components of business management.
Social marketing	Social marketing is the systematic application of marketing, along with other concepts and techniques, to achieve specific behavioral goals for a social good. Social marketing can be applied to promote merit goods, or to make a society avoid demerit goods and thus to promote society's well being as a whole. For example, this may include asking people not to smoke in public areas, asking them to use seat belts, or prompting to make them follow speed limits.
Public health	Public health is 'the science and art of preventing disease, prolonging life and promoting health through the organized efforts and informed choices of society, organizations, public and private, communities and individuals' (1920, C.E.A. Winslow). It is concerned with threats to health based on population health analysis. The population in question can be as small as a handful of people or as large as all the inhabitants of several continents (for instance, in the case of a pandemic).
Intervention	An intervention is an orchestrated attempt by one or many, people - usually family and friends - to get someone to seek professional help with an addiction or some kind of traumatic event or crisis, or other serious problem. The term intervention is most often used when the traumatic event involves addiction to drugs or other items. Intervention can also refer to the act of using a similar technique within a therapy session.
Primary care	Primary care is the health care given by a health care provider. Typically this provider acts as the principal point of consultation for patients within a health care system and coordinates other specialists that the patient may need.

7. HEALTH AND BEHAVIOR

Institution	An institution is any structure or mechanism of social order and cooperation governing the behavior of a set of individuals within a given human community. Institutions are identified with a social purpose and permanence, transcending individual human lives and intention by enforcing rules that governs cooperative human behavior. The term 'institution' is commonly applied to customs and behavior patterns important to a society, as well as to particular formal organizations of government and public service.
Social ecological model	The Social Ecology Model, also called Social Ecological Perspective, is a framework to examine the multiple effects and interrelatedness of social elements in an environment. Social ecological model can provide a theoretical framework to analyze various contexts in multiple types of research and in conflict communication (Oetzel, Ting-Toomey, & Rinderle, 2006). Social ecology is the study of people in an environment and the influences on one another (Hawley, 1950).
Policy	A policy is typically described as a principle or rule to guide decisions and achieve rational outcomes. The term is not normally used to denote what is actually done, this is normally referred to as either procedure or protocol. Policies are generally adopted by the Board of or senior governance body within an organization whereas procedures or protocols would be developed and adopted by senior executive officers.
Control	Controlling is ones of the managerial functions like planning, organizing, staffing and directing. It is an important function because it helps to check the errors and to take the corrective action so that deviation from standards are minimized and stated goals of the organization are achieved in desired manner.According to modern concepts, control is a foreseeing action whereas earlier concept of control was used only when errors were detected. Control in management means setting standards, measuring actual performance and taking corrective action.
Childhood obesity	Childhood obesity is a condition where excess body fat negatively affects a child's health or wellbeing. As methods to determine body fat directly are difficult, the diagnosis of obesity is often based on BMI. Due to the rising prevalence of obesity in children and its many adverse health effects it is being recognized as a serious public health concern. The term overweight rather than obese is often used in children as it is less stigmatizing.
Consolidated Omnibus Budget Reconciliation Act	The Consolidated Omnibus Budget Reconciliation Act of 1985, is a law passed by the U.S. Congress and signed by President Reagan that, among other things, mandates an insurance program giving some employees the ability to continue health insurance coverage after leaving employment. Consolidated Omnibus Budget Reconciliation Act includes amendments to the Employee Retirement Income Security Act of 1974 (ERISA).

Safeword	A Safeword is a codeword) to unambiguously communicate their physical or emotional state to a dominant (or 'top'), typically when approaching, or crossing, a physical, emotional, or moral boundary. Some Safewords are used to stop the scene outright, while others can communicate a willingness to continue, but at a reduced level of intensity. Safewords are agreed upon before playing a scene by all participants.
Crossing the Quality Chasm	Crossing the Quality Chasm: A New Health System for the 21st Century The committee on the Quality of Health Care in America released this report on March 1, 2001. It followed the 1999 report, To Err is Human: Building a Safer Health System, which brought to light the human toll and financial cost of medical error. These two documents were instrumental in raising patient safety to a major concern in health care and among policymakers. This report urgently calls for change to the health care system processes to improve the level of quality.
Chronic	A chronic condition is a human health condition or disease that is persistent or otherwise long-lasting in its effects. The term chronic is usually applied when the course of the disease lasts for more than three months. Common chronic diseases include arthritis, asthma, cancer, COPD, diabetes and HIV/AIDS. In medicine, the opposite of chronic is acute.
Chronic care	Chronic care refers to medical care which addresses preexisting or long term illness, as opposed to acute care which is concerned with short term or severe illness of brief duration. Chronic medical conditions include, but are not limited to, asthma, emphysema, chronic bronchitis, congestive heart disease, cirrhosis of the liver, hypertension and depression. Chronic medical care accounts for more than 75% of health care dollars spent in the US. Nursing care for the chronically ill A nurse has to be qualified to handle all the needs of a chronic client.
Health care	Health care is the diagnosis, treatment, and prevention of disease, illness, injury, and other physical and mental impairments in humans. Health care is delivered by practitioners in medicine, chiropractic, dentistry, nursing, pharmacy, allied health, and other care providers. It refers to the work done in providing primary care, secondary care and tertiary care, as well as in public health.
Medi-Cal	The California Medical Assistance Program (Medi-Cal is the name of the California Medicaid welfare program serving low-income families, seniors, persons with disabilities, children in foster care, pregnant women, and certain low-income adults. It is jointly administered by the California Department of Health Care Services (DHCS) and the Centers for Medicare and Medicaid Services (CMS), with many services implemented at the local level mainly by the counties of California.

7. HEALTH AND BEHAVIOR

Medical home	The medical home, is a team based health care delivery model led by a physician that provides comprehensive and continuous medical care to patients with the goal of obtaining maximized health outcomes (American College of Physicians) (American Academy of Family Physicians). It is 'an approach to providing comprehensive primary care for children, youth and adults'. The provision of medical homes may allow better access to health care, increase satisfaction with care, and improve health.
Copayment	In the United States, copayment is accessed. It is technically a form of coinsurance, but is defined differently in health insurance where a coinsurance is a percentage payment after the deductible up to a certain limit. It must be paid before any policy benefit is payable by an insurance company.
Paradigm	In the behavioural sciences, e.g. Psychology, Biology, Neurosciences, an experimental paradigm is an experimental setup (i.e. a way to conduct a certain type of experiment) that is defined by certain fine-tuned standards and often has a theoretical background. A paradigm in this technical sense, however, is not a way of thinking as it is in the epistemological meaning. See also: Paradigm, Design of experiments
Quality improvement	The term quality management has a specific meaning within many business sectors. This specific definition, which does not aim to assure 'good quality' by the more general definition, but rather to ensure that an organization or product is consistent, can be considered to have four main components: quality planning, quality control, quality assurance and quality improvement. Quality management is focused not only on product/service quality, but also the means to achieve it.
Trial	In law, a trial is when parties come together to a dispute present information (in the form of evidence) in a formal setting, usually a court, before a judge, jury, in order to achieve a resolution to their dispute. · Where the trial is held before a group of members of the community, it is called a jury trial. · Where the trial is held solely before a judge, it is called a bench trial. Bench trials involve fewer formalities, and are typically resolved faster. Furthermore, a favorable ruling for one party in a bench trial will frequently lead the other party to offer a settlement.
Initiative	An initiative represents an enterprise's readiness to embark on a new venture. Generally speaking, the motivation for an initiative arises from a desire to accomplish something that would benefit the enterprise, such as improving productivity, reducing costs or increasing market share. A typical initiative is expressed as a process and includes metrics and time frames.
Case study	A case study is an intensive analysis of an individual unit (e.g., a person, group, or event) stressing developmental factors in relation to context. The case study is common in social sciences and life sciences.

1. The _____, is a team based health care delivery model led by a physician that provides comprehensive and continuous medical care to patients with the goal of obtaining maximized health outcomes (American College of Physicians) (American Academy of Family Physicians). It is 'an approach to providing comprehensive primary care for children, youth and adults'. The provision of _____s may allow better access to health care, increase satisfaction with care, and improve health.

    a. Medication Administration Record
    b. Medical home
    c. Monitoring
    d. Monthly Prescribing Reference

2. A _____ is a codeword) to unambiguously communicate their physical or emotional state to a dominant (or 'top'), typically when approaching, or crossing, a physical, emotional, or moral boundary. Some _____s are used to stop the scene outright, while others can communicate a willingness to continue, but at a reduced level of intensity.

    _____s are agreed upon before playing a scene by all participants.

    a. 19NorDehydroepiandrosterone
    b. Comfort food
    c. Safeword
    d. Diet-induced obese

3. The California Medical Assistance Program (_____ is the name of the California Medicaid welfare program serving low-income families, seniors, persons with disabilities, children in foster care, pregnant women, and certain low-income adults. It is jointly administered by the California Department of Health Care Services (DHCS) and the Centers for Medicare and Medicaid Services (CMS), with many services implemented at the local level mainly by the counties of California. Approximately 8.8 million citizens were enrolled in _____ for at least 1 month in 2009-10, or about 23% of California's population.

    a. Medi-Cal
    b. Medically Unlikely Edit
    c. Medicare Advantage
    d. Medicare and Medicaid Extenders Act of 2010

4. _____ is an agricultural product processed from the leaves of plants in the genus Nicotiana. It can be consumed, used as a pesticide and, in the form of nicotine tartrate, used in some medicines. It is most commonly used as a drug, and is a valuable cash crop for countries such as Cuba, India, China, and the United States.

    a. Yerba mate
    b. 19NorDehydroepiandrosterone
    c. Tobacco
    d. 21-Hydroxylase

5. . The term quality management has a specific meaning within many business sectors.

This specific definition, which does not aim to assure 'good quality' by the more general definition, but rather to ensure that an organization or product is consistent, can be considered to have four main components: quality planning, quality control, quality assurance and _____. Quality management is focused not only on product/service quality, but also the means to achieve it.

a. Quality improvement
b. Placebo-controlled study
c. Pooling design
d. Provocation test

1. b
2. c
3. a
4. c
5. a

You can take the complete Online Interactive Chapter Practice Test

for 7. HEALTH AND BEHAVIOR
on all key terms, persons, places, and concepts.

No Additional Costs

http://www.Cram101.com

Register, send an email request to Travis.Reese@Cram101.com to get your user Id and password.

Include your customer order number, and ISBN number from your studyguide Retailer.

8. VULNERABLE POPULATIONS: A TALE OF TWO NATIONS

CHAPTER OUTLINE: KEY TERMS, PEOPLE, PLACES, CONCEPTS

	Medicare
	RECOrd
	Initiative
	Health
	Service
	Environmental enrichment
	Risk
	Risk factor
	Group Health
	Health Center
	Enabling
	Social capital
	Chronic
	Income
	Nutrition
	Supplemental Nutrition Assistance Program
	Combat Support Hospital
	Public hospital
	Underinsurance
	Department of Health and Human Services
	Federally Qualified Health Center

	Cranial root of accessory nerve
	Clinic
	Community health
	Community health center
	Accreditation
	Indian Health Service
	Public health
	Health care
	Nurse Practitioner
	Primary care
	Rural health
	Rural health clinic
	Dependency
	Mental health
	Food
	Supplemental Security Income
	Temporary Assistance for Needy Families
	Human services
	Disproportionate share hospital
	Preventive care
	Intermountain Healthcare

CHAPTER OUTLINE: KEY TERMS, PEOPLE, PLACES, CONCEPTS

	Coalition
	Electronic health record
	Health record
	Integrated care
	Social services

CHAPTER HIGHLIGHTS & NOTES: KEY TERMS, PEOPLE, PLACES, CONCEPTS

Medicare	Medicare is the unofficial name for Canada's publicly funded universal health insurance system. The formal terminology for the insurance system is provided by the Canada Health Act and the health insurance legislation of the individual provinces and territories. Under the terms of the Canada Health Act, all 'insured persons' (basically, legal residents of Canada, including permanent residents) are entitled to receive 'insured services' without copayment.
RECOrd	RECOrd is a Local Biological Records Centre (LRC) serving Cheshire, Halton, Warrington and Wirral (including the vice-county 'pan-handle' boundary around Stockport) - 'The Cheshire region'. It provides a local facility for the storage, validation and usage of Cheshire-based biological data under the National Biodiversity Network (NBN) project. It is one of a number of local Biological Records Centres across Britain which together aim to give complete geographic coverage of the UK. The organisation is housed in Oakfield House at Chester Zoo.
Initiative	An initiative represents an enterprise's readiness to embark on a new venture. Generally speaking, the motivation for an initiative arises from a desire to accomplish something that would benefit the enterprise, such as improving productivity, reducing costs or increasing market share. A typical initiative is expressed as a process and includes metrics and time frames.
Health	Health is the level of functional or metabolic efficiency of a living being.

8. VULNERABLE POPULATIONS: A TALE OF TWO NATIONS

	In humans, it is the general condition of a person's mind and body, usually meaning to be free from illness, injury or pain (as in 'good health' or 'healthy'). The World Health Organization (WHO) defined health in its broader sense in 1946 as 'a state of complete physical, mental, and social well-being and not merely the absence of disease or infirmity.' Although this definition has been subject to controversy, in particular as lacking operational value and because of the problem created by use of the word 'complete', it remains the most enduring .
Service	In economics, a service is an intangible commodity. More specifically, services are an intangible equivalent of economic goods. Service provision is often an economic activity where the buyer does not generally, except by exclusive contract, obtain exclusive ownership of the thing purchased.
Environmental enrichment	Environmental enrichment concerns how the brain is affected by the stimulation of its information processing provided by its surroundings (including the opportunity to interact socially). Brains in richer, more stimulating environments, have increased numbers of synapses, and the dendrite arbors upon which they reside are more complex. This effect happens particularly during neurodevelopment, but also to a lesser degree in adulthood.
Risk	Risk is the potential that a chosen action or activity (including the choice of inaction) will lead to a loss (an undesirable outcome). The notion implies that a choice having an influence on the outcome sometimes exists . Potential losses themselves may also be called 'risks'.
Risk factor	In epidemiology, a risk factor is a variable associated with an increased risk of disease or infection. Sometimes, determinant is also used, being a variable associated with either increased or decreased risk. Risk factors or determinants are correlational and not necessarily causal, because correlation does not prove causation.
Group Health	Group Health Cooperative, more commonly known as Group Health, is a Seattle, Washington based nonprofit healthcare organization. Established in 1945, it today provides coverage and care for about 700,000 people in Washington and Idaho and is one of the largest private employers in Washington. Patients who receive care at its medical centers are provided Web access to their medical records, secure emailing with doctors and nurses and the ability to fill prescriptions online that are mailed to homes without a shipping charge.
Health Center	A health center is a clinic staffed by a group of general practitioners and nurses. Typical services covered are family practice and dental care, but some clinics have expanded greatly and can include internal medicine, pediatric, women's care, family planning, pharmacy, lab, and more. Community Health Centers (CHCs) in the U.S.

Enabling	Enabling is a term with a double meaning.
	As a positive term, it references patterns of interaction which allow individuals to develop and grow. These may be on any scale, for example within the family, or in wider society as 'Enabling acts' designed to empower some group, or create a new authority for a (usually governmental) body.
Social capital	In sociology, social capital is the expected collective or economic benefits derived from the preferential treatment and cooperation between individuals and groups. Although different social sciences emphasize different aspects of social capital, they tend to share the core idea 'that social networks have value'. Just as a screwdriver (physical capital) or a university education (cultural capital or human capital) can increase productivity (both individual and collective), so do social contacts affect the productivity of individuals and groups.
Chronic	A chronic condition is a human health condition or disease that is persistent or otherwise long-lasting in its effects. The term chronic is usually applied when the course of the disease lasts for more than three months. Common chronic diseases include arthritis, asthma, cancer, COPD, diabetes and HIV/AIDS.
	In medicine, the opposite of chronic is acute.
Income	Income is the consumption and savings opportunity gained by an entity within a specified timeframe, which is generally expressed in monetary terms. However, for households and individuals, 'income is the sum of all the wages, salaries, profits, interests payments, rents and other forms of earnings received... in a given period of time.'
	In the field of public economics, the term may refer to the accumulation of both monetary and non-monetary consumption ability, with the former (monetary) being used as a proxy for total income. Increase in income
	Income per capita has been increasing steadily in almost every country.
Nutrition	Nutrition is the provision, to cells and organisms, of the materials necessary (in the form of food) to support life. Many common health problems can be prevented or alleviated with a healthy diet.
	The diet of an organism is what it eats, which is largely determined by the perceived palatability of foods.
Supplemental Nutrition Assistance Program	The United States Supplemental Nutrition Assistance Program , historically and commonly known as the Food Stamp Program, is a federal-assistance program that provides assistance to low- and no-income people and families living in the U.S. Though the program is administered by the U.S. Department of Agriculture, benefits are distributed by the individual U.S. states.

	Today, most food-stamp benefits are now distributed using cards but for most of its history the program had actually used paper denominational stamps/ coupons worth US$1, US$5, and US$10. These stamps could be used to purchase any prepackaged edible foods regardless of nutritional value (for example soft drinks and confectionery could be purchased on food stamps). In the late 1990s, the food-stamp program was revamped and actual stamps were phased out in favor of a specialized debit-card system known as Electronic Benefit Transfer (EBT) provided by private contractors.
Combat Support Hospital	A Combat Support Hospital is a type of field hospital. The Combat Support Hospital is a United States military mobile hospital delivered to the Corps Support Area in standard military-owned Demountable Containers (MILVAN) cargo containers and assembled by the staff into a tent hospital to treat wounded soldiers. The size of the hospital is almost infinitely expandable by chaining tents together, but it will typically deploy with between 16 and 256 operational hospital beds.
Public hospital	A public hospital is owned by a government and receives government funding. This type of hospital provides medical care free of charge, the cost of which is covered by the funding the hospital receives. Australia In Australia, public hospitals are operated and funded by each individual state's health department.
Underinsurance	Condition of average (also called underinsurance in the U.S., or principal of average, subject to average, or pro rata condition of average in Commonwealth countries) is the insurance term used when calculating a payout against a claim where the policy undervalues the sum insured. In the event of partial loss, the amount paid against a claim will be in the same proportion as the value of the underinsurance. The formula used is where Payout is the amount paid out by the policy, Claim is the amount claimed against the policy after a loss, Sum Insured is the maximum amount to be paid out by the policy, and Current Value is the value the policy should be insured for.
Department of Health and Human Services	The United States Department of Health and Human Services (HHS) is a Cabinet department of the United States government with the goal of protecting the health of all Americans and providing essential human services. Its motto is 'Improving the health, safety, and well-being of America'. Before its education functions were spun off in 1979, it was called the Department of Health, Education, and Welfare. · 1 History · 2 Agencies

· 2.1 Office of the Secretary (OS) · 2.2 Operating divisions · 3

· Immediate Office of the Secretary (IOS) - currently led by Kathleen Sebelius · Office of the Deputy Secretary (DS) - currently led by Deputy Secretary Bill Corr · Assistant Secretary for Administration and Management (ASAM)

· Program Support Center (PSC) - currently led by Director Philip Van Landingham · Assistant Secretary for Legislation (ASL) · Assistant Secretary for Planning and Evaluation (ASPE) · Assistant Secretary for Preparedness and Response (ASPR)

· Biomedical Advanced Research and Development Authority (BARDA)

· Project BioShield · Public Health Emergency Medical Countermeasures Enterprise (PHEMCE) · Assistant Secretary for Public Affairs (ASPA) · Assistant Secretary for Resources and Technology (ASRT) · Departmental Appeals Board (DAB) · Office for Civil Rights (OCR) · Office of Global Health Affairs (OGHA) · Office of Intergovernmental Affairs (IGA) · Office of the Secretary's Regional Directors · Office of the General Counsel (OGC) · Office of Inspector General (OIG) - currently led by Inspector General Daniel R. Levinson · Office of Medicare Hearings and Appeals (OMHA) · Office of the National Coordinator for Health Information Technology (ONC) · Public Health Service (PHS) / Office of the Assistant Secretary for Health (ASH) - currently led by Assistant Secretary, Howard K. Koh

· Office of Public Health and Science (OPHS) · Office of the Surgeon General - currently led by Acting Surgeon General, Rear Admiral Steven K. Galson

· U.S. Public Health Service (USPHS) Commissioned Corps · Office on Disability (OD - currently led by Director Henry Claypool · Center for Faith-Based and Community Initiatives (CFBCI)

· Administration for Children and Families (ACF) - currently led by Principal Deputy Assistant Secretary David Hansell · Administration on Aging (AoA) - currently led by Assistant Secretary Kathy Greenlee · Agency for Healthcare Research and Quality (AHRQ) - currently led by Director Carolyn Clancy · Agency for Toxic Substances and Disease Registry (ATSDR) - currently led by Administrator Thomas R. Frieden · Centers for Disease Control and Prevention (CDC) - currently led by Director Thomas R. Frieden · Centers for Medicare and Medicaid Services (CMS)- currently led by Acting Administrator Charlene Frizzera · Food and Drug Administration (FDA) - currently led by Commissioner Margaret Hamburg · Health Resources and Services Administration (HRSA) - currently led by Administrator Mary Wakefield · Indian Health Service (IHS) - currently led by Acting Director, Robert G. McSwain · National Institutes of Health (NIH) - currently led by Director Francis Collins · Substance Abuse and Mental Health Services Administration (SAMHSA) - currently led by Administrator Charles Curie

(Several agencies within HHS are components of the Public Health Service (PHS), including AHRQ, ASPR, ATSDR, CDC, FDA, HRSA, IHS, NIH, SAMHSA, OGHA, and OPHS).

· Social Security Administration, made independent in 1995. · Health Care Financing Administration

The Department of Health and Human Services' budget includes more than 300 programs, covering a wide spectrum of activities. Some highlights include:

· Health and social science research · Preventing disease, including immunization services · Assuring food and drug safety · Medicare (health insurance for elderly and disabled Americans) and Medicaid (health insurance for low-income people) · Health information technology · Financial assistance and services for low-income families · Improving maternal and infant health, including a Nurse Home Visitation to support first-time mothers. · Head Start (pre-school education and services) · Faith-based and community initiatives · Preventing child abuse and domestic violence · Substance abuse treatment and prevention · Services for older Americans, including home-delivered meals · Comprehensive health services for Native Americans · Medical preparedness for emergencies, including potential terrorism.

Federally Qualified Health Center	A Federally Qualified Health Center is a reimbursement designation from the Bureau of Primary Health Care and the Centers for Medicare and Medicaid Services of the United States Department of Health and Human Services. This designation is significant for several health programs funded under the Health Center Consolidation Act (Section 330 of the Public Health Service Act). Funded programs Health programs funded include:•Community Health Centers which serve a variety of Federally designated Medically Underserved Area/Populations (MUA or MUP)•Migrant Health Centers which provide culturally-competent and primary preventive medical care to migrant and seasonal agricultural workers,•Health Care for the Homeless Programs which reach out to homeless individuals and families and provide primary and preventive care and substance abuse services, and•Public Housing Primary Care Programs that serve residents of public housing and are located in or adjacent to the communities they serve Federally Qualified Health Centers are community-based organizations that provide comprehensive primary care and preventive care, including health, oral, and mental healthsubstance abuse services to persons of all ages, regardless of their ability to pay or health insurance status.
Cranial root of accessory nerve	The cranial root of accessory nerve is the smaller of the two portions of the accessory nerve. It is generally considered as a part of the vagus nerve and not part of the accessory nerve proper because the cranial component rapidly joins the vagus nerve and serves the same function as other vagal nerve fibers.

Clinic	A clinic (or outpatient clinic is primarily devoted to the care of outpatients. Clinics can be privately operated or publicly managed and funded, and typically cover the primary health care needs of populations in local communities, in contrast to larger hospitals which offer specialized treatments and admit inpatients for overnight stays. Some clinics grow to be institutions as large as major hospitals, or become associated with a hospital or medical school, while retaining the name 'clinic'.
Community health	Community health, a field within public health, is a discipline that concerns itself with the study and betterment of the health characteristics of biological communities. While the term community can be broadly defined, Community health tends to focus on geographic areas rather than people with shared characteristics. The health characteristics of a community are often examined using geographic information system (GIS) software and public health datasets.
Community health center	A health center or community health center is a clinic staffed by a group of general practitioners and nurses. Typical services covered are family practice and dental care, but some clinics have expanded greatly and can include internal medicine, pediatric, women's care, family planning, pharmacy, lab, and more. Community Health Centers in the U.S. are neighborhood health centers generally serving Medically Underserved Areas (MUAs) which includes persons who are uninsured, underinsured, low-income or those living in areas where little access to primary health care is available.
Accreditation	Accreditation is a process in which certification of competency, authority, or credibility is presented. Organizations that issue credentials or certify third parties against official standards are themselves formally accredited by accreditation bodies (such as UKAS); hence they are sometimes known as 'accredited certification bodies'. The accreditation process ensures that their certification practices are acceptable, typically meaning that they are competent to test and certify third parties, behave ethically and employ suitable quality assurance.
Indian Health Service	The Indian Health Service is an operating division (OPDIV) within the U.S. Department of Health and Human Services (HHS). Indian Health Service is responsible for providing medical and public health services to members of federally recognized Tribes and Alaska Natives. Indian Health Service is the principal federal health care provider and health advocate for Indian people, and its goal is to raise their health status to the highest possible level.
Public health	Public health is 'the science and art of preventing disease, prolonging life and promoting health through the organized efforts and informed choices of society, organizations, public and private, communities and individuals' (1920, C.E.A. Winslow). It is concerned with threats to health based on population health analysis. The population in question can be as small as a handful of people or as large as all the inhabitants of several continents (for instance, in the case of a pandemic).

8. VULNERABLE POPULATIONS: A TALE OF TWO NATIONS

Health care	Health care is the diagnosis, treatment, and prevention of disease, illness, injury, and other physical and mental impairments in humans. Health care is delivered by practitioners in medicine, chiropractic, dentistry, nursing, pharmacy, allied health, and other care providers. It refers to the work done in providing primary care, secondary care and tertiary care, as well as in public health.
Nurse Practitioner	A Nurse Practitioner is an Advanced Practice Nurse (APN) who has completed graduate-level education (either a Master's or a Doctoral degree). Additional APN roles include the Certified Registered Nurse Anesthetist (CRNA)s, CNMs, and CNSs. All Nurse Practitioners are Registered Nurses who have completed extensive additional education, training, and have a dramatically expanded scope of practice over the traditional RN role.
Primary care	Primary care is the health care given by a health care provider. Typically this provider acts as the principal point of consultation for patients within a health care system and coordinates other specialists that the patient may need. Such a professional can be a primary care physician, such as a general practitioner or family physician, or depending on the locality, health system organization, and patient's discretion, they may see a pharmacist, a physician assistant, a nurse practitioner, a nurse (such as in the United Kingdom), a clinical officer (such as in parts of Africa), or an Ayurvedic or other traditional medicine professional (such as in parts of Asia).
Rural health	In medicine, rural health is the interdisciplinary study of health and health care delivery in the context of a rural environment or location. Some of the fields of study comprising rural health include: health, geography, midwifery, nursing, sociology, economics, and telehealthtelemedicine. The term 'rural' can be defined in many ways, such as by population density, by geographic location or other factors.
Rural health clinic	A Rural Health Clinic is a clinic located in a rural, medically under-served area in the United States that has a separate reimbursement structure from the standard medical office under the Medicare and Medicaid programs. Rural health clinics were established by the Rural Health Clinics Act (P.L. 95-210), (Section 1905 of the Social Security Act). The program was established to address an inadequate supply of physicians serving Medicare beneficiaries and Medicaid recipients in rural areas and to increase the utilization of non-physician practitioners.
Dependency	In a project network, a dependency is a link amongst a project's terminal elements. There are four kinds of dependencies with respect to ordering terminal elements (in order of decreasing frequency of use):•Finish to start (FS) •A FS B = B can't start before A is finished•• (Foundations dug) FS (Concrete poured)•Finish to finish (FF) •A FF B = B can't finish before A is finished••(Last chapter written) FF (Entire book written)•Start to start (SS). •A SS B = B can't start before A starts••(Project work started) SS (Project management activities started)•Start to finish (SF) •A SF B = B can't finish before A starts••(New shift started) SF (Previous shift finished)

| Mental health | Mental health is a term used to describe either a level of cognitive or emotional well-being or an absence of a mental disorder. From perspectives of the discipline of positive psychology or holism Mental health may include an individual's ability to enjoy life and procure a balance between life activities and efforts to achieve psychological resilience.

The World Health Organization defines Mental health as 'a state of well-being in which the individual realizes his or her own abilities, can cope with the normal stresses of life, can work productively and fruitfully, and is able to make a contribution to his or her community'. |
| --- | --- |
| Food | Food is any substance consumed to provide nutritional support for the body. It is usually of plant or animal origin, and contains essential nutrients, such as carbohydrates, fats, proteins, vitamins, or minerals. The substance is ingested by an organism and assimilated by the organism's cells in an effort to produce energy, maintain life, or stimulate growth. |
| Supplemental Security Income | Supplemental Security Income is a United States government program that provides stipends to low-income people who are either aged (65 or older), blind, or disabled. Although administered by the Social Security Administration, SSI is funded from the U.S. Treasury general funds, not the Social Security trust fund. SSI was created in 1974 to replace federal-state adult assistance programs that served the same purpose. |
| Temporary Assistance for Needy Families | Temporary Assistance for Needy Families is one of the United States of America's federal assistance programs. It began on July 1, 1997, and succeeded the Aid to Families with Dependent Children (AFDC) program, providing cash assistance to indigent American families with dependent children through the United States Department of Health and Human Services.

TANF was created by the Personal Responsibility and Work Opportunity Act instituted under President Bill Clinton in 1996. The Act provides temporary financial assistance while aiming to get people off of that assistance, primarily through employment. |
| Human services | Human services refers to a variety of delivery systems such as social welfare services, education, mental health services, and other forms of healthcare. Human services professionals may provide services directly to clients or help clients access services. Human services professionals also manage agencies that provide these services. |
| Disproportionate share hospital | The United States government provides funding to hospitals that treat indigent patients through the Disproportionate Share Hospital programs, under which facilities are able to receive at least partial compensation.

Although 3,109 hospitals receive this adjustment, Medicare Disproportionate share hospital payments are highly concentrated. |

8. VULNERABLE POPULATIONS: A TALE OF TWO NATIONS

Preventive care	Preventive care is a set of measures taken in advance of symptoms to prevent illness or injury. This type of care is best exemplified by routine physical examinations and immunizations. The emphasis is on preventing illnesses before they occur.
Intermountain Healthcare	Intermountain Health Care, Inc., officially doing business as as Intermountain Healthcare, is a non-profit healthcare system and is the largest healthcare provider in the Intermountain West. Until 2005 it known as Intermountain Health Care or more commonly IHC; it is now. Intermountain Healthcare is headquartered in Salt Lake City, Utah, and currently employs over 32,000 people.
Coalition	A coalition is an alliance among individuals or groups, during which they cooperate in joint action, each in his own self-interest, joining forces together for a common cause. This alliance may be temporary or a matter of convenience. A coalition thus differs from a more formal covenant.
Electronic health record	An electronic health record is an evolving concept defined as a systematic collection of electronic health information about individual patients or populations. It is a record in digital format that is theoretically capable of being shared across different health care settings. In some cases this sharing can occur by way of network-connected enterprise-wide information systems and other information networks or exchanges.
Health record	The terms medical record, health record, and medical chart are used somewhat interchangeably to describe the systematic documentation of a single patient's medical history and care across time within one particular health care provider's jurisdiction. The medical record includes a variety of types of 'notes' entered over time by health care professionals, recording observations and administration of drugs and therapies, orders for the administration of drugs and therapies, test results, x-rays, reports, etc. The maintenance of complete and accurate medical records is a requirement of health care providers and is generally enforced as a licensing or certification prerequisite.
Integrated care	Integrated care - also known as coordinated care, comprehensive care, seamless care and transmural care - is a worldwide trend in health care reforms and new organizational arrangements focusing on more coordinated and integrated forms of care provision. Integrated care may be seen as a response to the fragmented delivery of health and social services being an acknowledged problem in many health systems. Integrated care covers a complex and comprehensive field and there are many different approaches to and definitions of the concept.
Social services	Social services are a range of public services provided by many national or regional government organisation for its residents, including such things as healthcare, public housing, and social security.

1. _____ Cooperative, more commonly known as _____, is a Seattle, Washington based nonprofit healthcare organization. Established in 1945, it today provides coverage and care for about 700,000 people in Washington and Idaho and is one of the largest private employers in Washington. Patients who receive care at its medical centers are provided Web access to their medical records, secure emailing with doctors and nurses and the ability to fill prescriptions online that are mailed to homes without a shipping charge.

   a. 19NorDehydroepiandrosterone
   b. Sensitivity and specificity
   c. Group Health
   d. Surrogate endpoint

2. _____ is any substance consumed to provide nutritional support for the body. It is usually of plant or animal origin, and contains essential nutrients, such as carbohydrates, fats, proteins, vitamins, or minerals. The substance is ingested by an organism and assimilated by the organism's cells in an effort to produce energy, maintain life, or stimulate growth.

   a. Food
   b. Culinary name
   c. Dish
   d. Fake food

3. _____ is the provision, to cells and organisms, of the materials necessary (in the form of food) to support life. Many common health problems can be prevented or alleviated with a healthy diet.

   The diet of an organism is what it eats, which is largely determined by the perceived palatability of foods.

   a. Pollutant Standards Index
   b. Race and health
   c. Rome Consensus for a Humanitarian Drug Policy
   d. Nutrition

4. In epidemiology, a _____ is a variable associated with an increased risk of disease or infection. Sometimes, determinant is also used, being a variable associated with either increased or decreased risk.

   _____s or determinants are correlational and not necessarily causal, because correlation does not prove causation.

   a. Rule of three
   b. Risk factor
   c. Standardized mortality ratio
   d. Surrogate endpoint

5. . _____ is one of the United States of America's federal assistance programs. It began on July 1, 1997, and succeeded the Aid to Families with Dependent Children (AFDC) program, providing cash assistance to indigent American families with dependent children through the United States Department of Health and Human Services.

TANF was created by the Personal Responsibility and Work Opportunity Act instituted under President Bill Clinton in 1996. The Act provides temporary financial assistance while aiming to get people off of that assistance, primarily through employment.

a. Abortion-breast cancer hypothesis
b. Temporary Assistance for Needy Families
c. TennCare
d. Tennessee Justice Center

ANSWER KEY
8. VULNERABLE POPULATIONS: A TALE OF TWO NATIONS

1. c
2. a
3. d
4. b
5. b

You can take the complete Online Interactive Chapter Practice Test

for 8. VULNERABLE POPULATIONS: A TALE OF TWO NATIONS
on all key terms, persons, places, and concepts.

No Additional Costs

http://www.Cram101.com

Register, send an email request to Travis.Reese@Cram101.com to get your user Id and password.

Include your customer order number, and ISBN number from your studyguide Retailer.

9. ORGANIZATION OF CARE

CHAPTER OUTLINE: KEY TERMS, PEOPLE, PLACES, CONCEPTS

_____ | Clinic

_____ | Adrenal gland disorders

_____ | Health

_____ | Health care

_____ | Service

_____ | Public health

_____ | Primary prevention

_____ | Tertiary

_____ | Tertiary prevention

_____ | Medicare

_____ | Acute

_____ | Acute care

_____ | Underinsurance

_____ | Medi-Cal

_____ | Urgent care

_____ | Whitehall Study

_____ | Chronic

_____ | Chronic care

_____ | Nurse Practitioner

_____ | Primary care

_____ | Specialty

Tertiary care

Inpatient care

Long-term care

Rehabilitation

Subacute

Income

Intermountain Healthcare

End-of-life care

Hospice

Hospice care

Outpatient

Palliative

Palliative care

Association

Health Officers

Accreditation

Consolidated Omnibus Budget Reconciliation Act

Psychiatric hospital

Rehabilitation hospital

Coalition

Ambulatory surgery

9. ORGANIZATION OF CARE

CHAPTER OUTLINE: KEY TERMS, PEOPLE, PLACES, CONCEPTS

	Ambulatory surgery centers
	Community health
	Community health center
	Health Center
	Assisted living
	Continuing care
	Independent living
	Nursing facility
	Retirement community
	Integrated delivery system
	Horizontal integration
	Vertical integration
	Safeword
	Crossing the Quality Chasm
	Health system
	Initiative
	Medical home
	Patient-centered care
	Patient-centered medical home
	Group Health

9. ORGANIZATION OF CARE

Clinic	A clinic (or outpatient clinic is primarily devoted to the care of outpatients. Clinics can be privately operated or publicly managed and funded, and typically cover the primary health care needs of populations in local communities, in contrast to larger hospitals which offer specialized treatments and admit inpatients for overnight stays. Some clinics grow to be institutions as large as major hospitals, or become associated with a hospital or medical school, while retaining the name 'clinic'.
Adrenal gland disorders	Adrenal gland disorders (or diseases) are conditions that interfere with the normal functioning of the adrenal glands. They are characterized by adrenal insufficiencies, where there are deficiencies in the availability of steroids that are produced by the adrenal glands. They may cause hyperfunction or hypofunction, and it may be congenital or acquired.
Health	Health is the level of functional or metabolic efficiency of a living being. In humans, it is the general condition of a person's mind and body, usually meaning to be free from illness, injury or pain (as in 'good health' or 'healthy'). The World Health Organization (WHO) defined health in its broader sense in 1946 as 'a state of complete physical, mental, and social well-being and not merely the absence of disease or infirmity.' Although this definition has been subject to controversy, in particular as lacking operational value and because of the problem created by use of the word 'complete', it remains the most enduring .
Health care	Health care is the diagnosis, treatment, and prevention of disease, illness, injury, and other physical and mental impairments in humans. Health care is delivered by practitioners in medicine, chiropractic, dentistry, nursing, pharmacy, allied health, and other care providers. It refers to the work done in providing primary care, secondary care and tertiary care, as well as in public health.
Service	In economics, a service is an intangible commodity. More specifically, services are an intangible equivalent of economic goods. Service provision is often an economic activity where the buyer does not generally, except by exclusive contract, obtain exclusive ownership of the thing purchased.
Public health	Public health is 'the science and art of preventing disease, prolonging life and promoting health through the organized efforts and informed choices of society, organizations, public and private, communities and individuals' (1920, C.E.A. Winslow). It is concerned with threats to health based on population health analysis. The population in question can be as small as a handful of people or as large as all the inhabitants of several continents (for instance, in the case of a pandemic).
Primary prevention	Primary prevention is any effort to avoid the development of a disease or condition.
Tertiary	The tertiary is a term for a geologic period 65 million to 1.8 million years ago. The tertiary covered the time span between the superseded Secondary period and an out-of-date definition of the Quaternary period.

Tertiary prevention	Tertiary prevention refers to treatment of a disease to avoid its worsening or the onset of any complications.
Medicare	Medicare is the unofficial name for Canada's publicly funded universal health insurance system. The formal terminology for the insurance system is provided by the Canada Health Act and the health insurance legislation of the individual provinces and territories. Under the terms of the Canada Health Act, all 'insured persons' (basically, legal residents of Canada, including permanent residents) are entitled to receive 'insured services' without copayment.
Acute	In medicine, an acute disease is a disease with either or both of:•a rapid onset, as in acute infection•a short course (as opposed to a chronic course). This adjective is part of the definition of several diseases and is, therefore, incorporated in their name, for instance, severe acute respiratory syndrome, acute leukemia. The term acute may often be confused by the general public to mean 'severe'. This however, is a different characteristic and something can be acute but not severe.
Acute care	Acute care is a branch of secondary health care where a patient receives active but short-term treatment for a severe injury or episode of illness, an urgent medical condition, or during recovery from surgery. In medical terms, care for acute health conditions is the opposite from chronic care, or longer term care. Acute care services are generally delivered by teams of health care professionals from a range of medical and surgical specialties.
Underinsurance	Condition of average (also called underinsurance in the U.S., or principal of average, subject to average, or pro rata condition of average in Commonwealth countries) is the insurance term used when calculating a payout against a claim where the policy undervalues the sum insured. In the event of partial loss, the amount paid against a claim will be in the same proportion as the value of the underinsurance. The formula used is where Payout is the amount paid out by the policy, Claim is the amount claimed against the policy after a loss, Sum Insured is the maximum amount to be paid out by the policy, and Current Value is the value the policy should be insured for.

9. ORGANIZATION OF CARE

Medi-Cal	The California Medical Assistance Program (Medi-Cal is the name of the California Medicaid welfare program serving low-income families, seniors, persons with disabilities, children in foster care, pregnant women, and certain low-income adults. It is jointly administered by the California Department of Health Care Services (DHCS) and the Centers for Medicare and Medicaid Services (CMS), with many services implemented at the local level mainly by the counties of California. Approximately 8.8 million citizens were enrolled in Medi-Cal for at least 1 month in 2009-10, or about 23% of California's population.
Urgent care	Urgent care is the delivery of ambulatory care in a facility dedicated to the delivery of medical care outside of a hospital emergency department, usually on an unscheduled, walk-in basis. Urgent care centers are primarily used to treat patients who have an injury or illness that requires immediate care but is not serious enough to warrant a visit to an emergency department. Often urgent care centers are not open on a continuous basis, unlike a hospital emergency department which would be open at all times.
Whitehall Study	The original Whitehall Study investigated social determinants of health, specifically the cardiorespiratory disease prevalence and mortality rates among British male civil servants between the ages of 20 and 64. The initial prospective cohort study, the Whitehall I Study, examined over 18,000 male civil servants, and was conducted over a period of ten years, beginning in 1967. A second cohort study, the Whitehall II Study, examined the health of 10,308 civil servants aged 35 to 55, of whom two thirds were men and one third women. The response rate for Whitehall II was 73% in total, 74% for men and 71% for women. A long-term follow-up of study subjects from the first two phases is ongoing.
Chronic	A chronic condition is a human health condition or disease that is persistent or otherwise long-lasting in its effects. The term chronic is usually applied when the course of the disease lasts for more than three months. Common chronic diseases include arthritis, asthma, cancer, COPD, diabetes and HIV/AIDS. In medicine, the opposite of chronic is acute.
Chronic care	Chronic care refers to medical care which addresses preexisting or long term illness, as opposed to acute care which is concerned with short term or severe illness of brief duration. Chronic medical conditions include, but are not limited to, asthma, emphysema, chronic bronchitis, congestive heart disease, cirrhosis of the liver, hypertension and depression. Chronic medical care accounts for more than 75% of health care dollars spent in the US. Nursing care for the chronically ill. A nurse has to be qualified to handle all the needs of a chronic client.
Nurse Practitioner	A Nurse Practitioner is an Advanced Practice Nurse (APN) who has completed graduate-level education (either a Master's or a Doctoral degree). Additional APN roles include the Certified Registered Nurse Anesthetist (CRNA)s, CNMs, and CNSs.

Primary care	Primary care is the health care given by a health care provider. Typically this provider acts as the principal point of consultation for patients within a health care system and coordinates other specialists that the patient may need. Such a professional can be a primary care physician, such as a general practitioner or family physician, or depending on the locality, health system organization, and patient's discretion, they may see a pharmacist, a physician assistant, a nurse practitioner, a nurse (such as in the United Kingdom), a clinical officer (such as in parts of Africa), or an Ayurvedic or other traditional medicine professional (such as in parts of Asia).
Specialty	A specialty in medicine is a branch of medical science. After completing medical school, physicians or surgeons usually further their medical education in a specific specialty of medicine by completing a multiple year residency to become a medical specialist. To a certain extent, medical practitioners have always been specialized.
Tertiary care	In medicine, tertiary care is specialized consultative care, usually on referral from primary or secondary medical care personnel, by specialists working in a center that has personnel and facilities for special investigation and treatment. Examples of tertiary care services are specialist cancer care, neurosurgery (brain surgery), burns care and plastic surgery.
Inpatient care	Inpatient care is the care of patients whose condition requires admission to a hospital. Progress in modern medicine and the advent of comprehensive out-patient clinics ensure that patients are only admitted to a hospital when they are extremely ill or are have severe physical trauma. Progress Patients enter inpatient care mainly from previous ambulatory care such as referral from a family doctor, or through emergency medicine departments.
Long-term care	Long-term care is a variety of services which help meet both the medical and non-medical needs of people with a chronic illness or disability who cannot care for themselves for long periods of time. It is common for long-term care to provide custodial and non-skilled care, such as assisting with normal daily tasks like dressing, bathing, and using the bathroom. Increasingly, long-term care involves providing a level of medical care that requires the expertise of skilled practitioners to address the often multiple chronic conditions associated with older populations.
Rehabilitation	Rehabilitation of sensory and cognitive function typically involves methods for retraining neural pathways or training new neural pathways to regain or improve neurocognitive functioning that has been diminished by disease or trauma Three common neuropsychological problems treatable with rehabilitation are attention deficit/hyperactivity disorder (ADHD), concussion, and spinal cord injury. Rehabilitation research and practices are a fertile area for clinical neuropsychologists and others.

9. ORGANIZATION OF CARE

Subacute	Subacute is defined as between acute and chronic, for example subacute fever symptoms or subacute endocarditis. An example is subacute sclerosing panencephalitis, a rare brain disease characterized by diminished intellectual function and loss of nervous function. Chronic is the opposite of acute - meaning a long term condition, for example chronic bronchitis.
Income	Income is the consumption and savings opportunity gained by an entity within a specified timeframe, which is generally expressed in monetary terms. However, for households and individuals, 'income is the sum of all the wages, salaries, profits, interests payments, rents and other forms of earnings received... in a given period of time.' In the field of public economics, the term may refer to the accumulation of both monetary and non-monetary consumption ability, with the former (monetary) being used as a proxy for total income. Increase in income Income per capita has been increasing steadily in almost every country.
Intermountain Healthcare	Intermountain Health Care, Inc., officially doing business as as Intermountain Healthcare, is a non-profit healthcare system and is the largest healthcare provider in the Intermountain West. Until 2005 it known as Intermountain Health Care or more commonly IHC; it is now. Intermountain Healthcare is headquartered in Salt Lake City, Utah, and currently employs over 32,000 people.
End-of-life care	In medicine, end-of-life care refers to medical care not only of patients in the final hours or days of their lives, but more broadly, medical care of all those with a terminal illness or terminal condition that has become advanced, progressive and incurable. Regarding cancer care the United States National Cancer Institute writes: When a patient's health care team determines that the cancer can no longer be controlled, medical testing and cancer treatment often stop. But the patient's care continues.
Hospice	Hospice is a type of care and a philosophy of care that focuses on the palliation of a terminally ill patient's symptoms. These symptoms can be physical, emotional, spiritual or social in nature. Hospice care focuses on bringing comfort, self-respect, and tranquility to the dying patient.
Hospice care	Hospice care is a type and philosophy of care that focuses on the palliative care of a terminally ill or seriously ill patient's pain and symptoms, and attending to their emotional and spiritual needs. Within the United States the term is largely defined by the practices of the Medicare system and other health insurance providers, which make hospice care available, either in an inpatient facility or at the patient's home, to patients with a terminal prognosis who are medically certified to have less than six months to live.

Outpatient	Outpatient refers to a patient who requires treatment but does not need to be admitted into the institution for those sevices.
Palliative	Palliative care is an area of healthcare that focuses on relieving and preventing the suffering of patients. Unlike hospice care, palliative medicine is appropriate for patients in all disease stages, including those undergoing treatment for curable illnesses and those living with chronic diseases, as well as patients who are nearing the end of life. Palliative medicine utilizes a multidisciplinary approach to patient care, relying on input from physicians, pharmacists, nurses, chaplains, social workers, psychologists, and other allied health professionals in formulating a plan of care to relieve suffering in all areas of a patient's life.
Palliative care	Palliative care is an area of healthcare that focuses on relieving and preventing the suffering of patients. Unlike hospice care, palliative medicine is appropriate for patients in all disease stages, including those undergoing treatment for curable illnesses and those living with chronic diseases, as well as patients who are nearing the end of life. Palliative medicine utilizes a multidisciplinary approach to patient care, relying on input from physicians, pharmacists, nurses, chaplains, social workers, psychologists, and other allied health professionals in formulating a plan of care to relieve suffering in all areas of a patient's life.
Association	In statistics, an association is any relationship between two measured quantities that renders them statistically dependent. The term 'association' refers broadly to any such relationship, whereas the narrower term 'correlation' refers to a linear relationship between two quantities. There are many statistical measures of association that can be used to infer the presence or absence of an association in a sample of data.
Health Officers	Health Officers Health Officers is a common term used in the United States and elsewhere for public health officials. Public health officials may serve at the global, federal, state, county, or municipal level. Health officers are concerned with protecting and improving the health of communities, states, nations and populations.
Accreditation	Accreditation is a process in which certification of competency, authority, or credibility is presented. Organizations that issue credentials or certify third parties against official standards are themselves formally accredited by accreditation bodies (such as UKAS); hence they are sometimes known as 'accredited certification bodies'. The accreditation process ensures that their certification practices are acceptable, typically meaning that they are competent to test and certify third parties, behave ethically and employ suitable quality assurance.

9. ORGANIZATION OF CARE

Consolidated Omnibus Budget Reconciliation Act	The Consolidated Omnibus Budget Reconciliation Act of 1985, is a law passed by the U.S. Congress and signed by President Reagan that, among other things, mandates an insurance program giving some employees the ability to continue health insurance coverage after leaving employment. Consolidated Omnibus Budget Reconciliation Act includes amendments to the Employee Retirement Income Security Act of 1974 (ERISA). The law deals with a great variety of subjects, such as tobacco price supports, railroads, private pension plans, disability insurance, and the postal service , but it is perhaps best known for Title X, which amends the Internal Revenue Code and the Public Health Service Act to deny income tax deductions to employers for contributions to a group health plan unless such plan meets certain continuing coverage requirements.
Psychiatric hospital	Psychiatric hospitals, also known as mental hospitals, are hospitals specializing in the treatment of serious mental disorders. Psychiatric hospitals vary widely in their size and grading. Some hospitals may specialise only in short-term or outpatient therapy for low-risk patients.
Rehabilitation hospital	A rehabilitation hospital, also referred to as Inpatient Rehabilitation Hospitals, are devoted to the rehabilitation of patients with various neurological, musculo-skeletal, orthopedic and other medical conditions following stabilization of their acute medical issues. The industry is largely made up by independent hospitals that operate these facilities within acute care hospitals. There are also Inpatient Rehabilitation Hospitals that offer this service in a hospital like setting, but separate from acute care facilities.
Coalition	A coalition is an alliance among individuals or groups, during which they cooperate in joint action, each in his own self-interest, joining forces together for a common cause. This alliance may be temporary or a matter of convenience. A coalition thus differs from a more formal covenant.
Ambulatory surgery	Outpatient surgery, also known as ambulatory surgery, same-day surgery or day surgery, is surgery that does not require an overnight hospital stay. The term "outpatient" arises from the fact that surgery patients may go home and do not need an overnight hospital bed. The purpose of outpatient surgery is to keep hospital costs down, as well as saving the patient time that would otherwise be wasted in the hospital.
Ambulatory surgery centers	Ambulatory surgery centers are also known as outpatient surgery centers or same day surgery centers. Medical facilities where surgical procedures not requiring an overnight hospital stay are performed are sometimes called surgicenters. Such surgery is commonly less complicated than that requiring hospitalization.
Community health	Community health, a field within public health, is a discipline that concerns itself with the study and betterment of the health characteristics of biological communities. While the term community can be broadly defined, Community health tends to focus on geographic areas rather than people with shared characteristics.

9. ORGANIZATION OF CARE

Community health center	A health center or community health center is a clinic staffed by a group of general practitioners and nurses. Typical services covered are family practice and dental care, but some clinics have expanded greatly and can include internal medicine, pediatric, women's care, family planning, pharmacy, lab, and more. Community Health Centers in the U.S. are neighborhood health centers generally serving Medically Underserved Areas (MUAs) which includes persons who are uninsured, underinsured, low-income or those living in areas where little access to primary health care is available.
Health Center	A health center is a clinic staffed by a group of general practitioners and nurses. Typical services covered are family practice and dental care, but some clinics have expanded greatly and can include internal medicine, pediatric, women's care, family planning, pharmacy, lab, and more. Community Health Centers (CHCs) in the U.S. are neighborhood health centers generally serving Medically Underserved Areas (MUAs) which includes persons who are uninsured, underinsured, low-income or those living in areas where little access to primary health care is available.
Assisted living	Assisted living residences or assisted living facilities (ALFs) provide supervision or assistance with activities of daily living (ADLs); coordination of services by outside health care providers; and monitoring of resident activities to help to ensure their health, safety, and well-being. Assistance may include the administration or supervision of medication, or personal care services provided by a trained staff person. Assisted living as it exists today emerged in the 1990s as an eldercare alternative on the continuum of care for people, normally seniors, for whom Independent living is no longer appropriate but who do not need the 24-hour medical care provided by a nursing home.
Continuing care	A Continuing care community is a type of retirement community where a number of aging care needs, from assisted living, independent living and nursing home care, may all be met in a single residence, whether apartment or enclosed unit. Typically, elderly candidates move into a continuing-care retirement community (Continuing careRC) while still living independently, with few health risks or healthcare needs, and will remain reside there until end of life. As patrons progress in age, and medical needs change, the level of nursing care and service increases proportionally in response.
Independent living	Independent living, as seen by its advocates, is a philosophy, a way of looking at disability and society, and a worldwide movement of people with disabilities working for self-determination, self-respect and equal opportunities. In the context of eldercare, independent living is seen as a step in the continuum of care, with assisted living being the next step.

9. ORGANIZATION OF CARE

Nursing facility	A nursing home, convalescent home, Skilled Nursing Unit (SNU), care home or rest home provides a type of care of residents: it is a place of residence for people who require constant nursing care and have significant deficiencies with activities of daily living. Residents include the elderly and younger adults with physical or mental disabilities. Eligible adults 18 or older can stay in a skilled Nursing facility to receive physical, occupational, and other rehabilitative therapies following an accident or illness.
Retirement community	A retirement community, is a very broad, generic term that covers many varieties of housing for retirees and seniors - especially designed or geared for people who no longer work, or restricted to those over a certain age. It differs from a retirement home which is a single building or small complex where no 'common areas' for socializing exist. Many retirement communities are planned for that purpose, and have special facilities catering to the needs and wants of retirees, including extensive amenities like clubhouses, swimming pools, arts and crafts, boating, trails, golf courses, active adult retail and on-site medical facilities.
Integrated delivery system	An integrated delivery system is a network of health care organizations under a parent holding company. Some Integrated delivery system have an HMO component, while others are a network of physicians only, or of physicians and hospitals. Thus, the term is used broadly to define an organization that provides a continuum of health care services.
Horizontal integration	In microeconomics and strategic management, the term horizontal integration describes a type of ownership and control. It is a strategy used by a business or corporation that seeks to sell a type of product in numerous markets. Horizontal integration in marketing is much more common than vertical integration is in production.
Vertical integration	In microeconomics and management, the term vertical integration describes a style of management control. Vertically integrated companies in a supply chain are united through a common owner. Usually each member of the supply chain produces a different product or (market-specific) service, and the products combine to satisfy a common need.
Safeword	A Safeword is a codeword) to unambiguously communicate their physical or emotional state to a dominant (or 'top'), typically when approaching, or crossing, a physical, emotional, or moral boundary. Some Safewords are used to stop the scene outright, while others can communicate a willingness to continue, but at a reduced level of intensity. Safewords are agreed upon before playing a scene by all participants.
Crossing the Quality Chasm	Crossing the Quality Chasm: A New Health System for the 21st Century The committee on the Quality of Health Care in America released this report on March 1, 2001. It followed the 1999 report, To Err is Human: Building a Safer Health System, which brought to light the human toll and financial cost of medical error.

	These two documents were instrumental in raising patient safety to a major concern in health care and among policymakers.
	This report urgently calls for change to the health care system processes to improve the level of quality.
Health system	A health system, also sometimes referred to as health care system or healthcare system is the organization of people, institutions, and resources to deliver health care services to meet the health needs of target populations.
	There is a wide variety of health systems around the world, with as many histories and organizational structures as there are nations. In some countries, health system planning is distributed among market participants.
Initiative	An initiative represents an enterprise's readiness to embark on a new venture. Generally speaking, the motivation for an initiative arises from a desire to accomplish something that would benefit the enterprise, such as improving productivity, reducing costs or increasing market share.
	A typical initiative is expressed as a process and includes metrics and time frames.
Medical home	The medical home, is a team based health care delivery model led by a physician that provides comprehensive and continuous medical care to patients with the goal of obtaining maximized health outcomes (American College of Physicians) (American Academy of Family Physicians). It is 'an approach to providing comprehensive primary care for children, youth and adults'. The provision of medical homes may allow better access to health care, increase satisfaction with care, and improve health.
Patient-centered care	Patient-centered care presumes active involvement of patients and their families in the design of new care models and in decision-making about individual options for treatment. Given that non-consumer stakeholders often don't know what matters most to patients regarding their ability to get and stay well, care that is truly patient-centered cannot be achieved without active patient engagement at every level of care design and implementation. The IOM (Institute of Medicine) defines patient-centered care as: Health care that establishes a partnership among practitioners, patients, and their families (when appropriate) to ensure that decisions respect patients' wants, needs, and preferences and that patients have the education and support they need to make decisions and participate in their own care.
Patient-centered medical home	The medical home, also known as the patient-centered medical home is a team based health care delivery model led by a physician, P.A., or N.P. that provides comprehensive and continuous medical care to patients with the goal of obtaining maximized health outcomes (American College of Physicians) (American Academy of Family Physicians). It is 'an approach to providing comprehensive primary care for children, youth and adults'.

9. ORGANIZATION OF CARE

Group Health	Group Health Cooperative, more commonly known as Group Health, is a Seattle, Washington based nonprofit healthcare organization. Established in 1945, it today provides coverage and care for about 700,000 people in Washington and Idaho and is one of the largest private employers in Washington. Patients who receive care at its medical centers are provided Web access to their medical records, secure emailing with doctors and nurses and the ability to fill prescriptions online that are mailed to homes without a shipping charge.

1. In economics, a _____ is an intangible commodity. More specifically, _____s are an intangible equivalent of economic goods.

   _____ provision is often an economic activity where the buyer does not generally, except by exclusive contract, obtain exclusive ownership of the thing purchased.

   a. Shipping list
   b. Stockout
   c. Service
   d. Supply chain

2. The _____ is a term for a geologic period 65 million to 1.8 million years ago. The _____ covered the time span between the superseded Secondary period and an out-of-date definition of the Quaternary period. The period began with the demise of the non-avian dinosaurs in the Cretaceous-_____ extinction event, at start of the Cenozoic era, spanning to beginning of the most recent Ice Age, at the end of the Pliocene epoch.

   a. Tertiary
   b. Board certification
   c. Brent Moelleken
   d. Center for the History of Family Medicine

3. . A _____ is a codeword) to unambiguously communicate their physical or emotional state to a dominant (or 'top'), typically when approaching, or crossing, a physical, emotional, or moral boundary. Some _____s are used to stop the scene outright, while others can communicate a willingness to continue, but at a reduced level of intensity.

   _____s are agreed upon before playing a scene by all participants.

   a. Safeword
   b. VRIO

c. Workplace strategy

d. Zaibatsu

4. A _____ in medicine is a branch of medical science. After completing medical school, physicians or surgeons usually further their medical education in a specific _____ of medicine by completing a multiple year residency to become a medical specialist.

To a certain extent, medical practitioners have always been specialized.

a. Biomedical scientist

b. Board certification

c. Center for the History of Family Medicine

d. Specialty

5. _____ is a branch of secondary health care where a patient receives active but short-term treatment for a severe injury or episode of illness, an urgent medical condition, or during recovery from surgery. In medical terms, care for acute health conditions is the opposite from chronic care, or longer term care.

_____ services are generally delivered by teams of health care professionals from a range of medical and surgical specialties.

a. Advanced paramedic

b. Acute care

c. AHRQ Health Care Innovations Exchange

d. ALOS

1. c
2. a
3. a
4. d
5. b

You can take the complete Online Interactive Chapter Practice Test

for 9. ORGANIZATION OF CARE
on all key terms, persons, places, and concepts.

No Additional Costs

http://www.Cram101.com

Register, send an email request to Travis.Reese@Cram101.com to get your user Id and password.

Include your customer order number, and ISBN number from your studyguide Retailer.

10. THE HEALTH WORKFORCE

_____ | Health

_____ | Health care

_____ | Income

_____ | Intermountain Healthcare

_____ | Interprofessional education

_____ | Bundled payment

_____ | Incentive

_____ | Human services

_____ | Service

_____ | Electronic health record

_____ | Health record

_____ | Information technology

_____ | Medi-Cal

_____ | Medical home

_____ | Nurse Practitioner

_____ | Patient-centered medical home

_____ | RECOrd

_____ | Kaiser Permanente

_____ | Case study

Health	Health is the level of functional or metabolic efficiency of a living being. In humans, it is the general condition of a person's mind and body, usually meaning to be free from illness, injury or pain (as in 'good health' or 'healthy'). The World Health Organization (WHO) defined health in its broader sense in 1946 as 'a state of complete physical, mental, and social well-being and not merely the absence of disease or infirmity.' Although this definition has been subject to controversy, in particular as lacking operational value and because of the problem created by use of the word 'complete', it remains the most enduring .
Health care	Health care is the diagnosis, treatment, and prevention of disease, illness, injury, and other physical and mental impairments in humans. Health care is delivered by practitioners in medicine, chiropractic, dentistry, nursing, pharmacy, allied health, and other care providers. It refers to the work done in providing primary care, secondary care and tertiary care, as well as in public health.
Income	Income is the consumption and savings opportunity gained by an entity within a specified timeframe, which is generally expressed in monetary terms. However, for households and individuals, 'income is the sum of all the wages, salaries, profits, interests payments, rents and other forms of earnings received... in a given period of time.' In the field of public economics, the term may refer to the accumulation of both monetary and non-monetary consumption ability, with the former (monetary) being used as a proxy for total income. Increase in income Income per capita has been increasing steadily in almost every country.
Intermountain Healthcare	Intermountain Health Care, Inc., officially doing business as as Intermountain Healthcare, is a non-profit healthcare system and is the largest healthcare provider in the Intermountain West. Until 2005 it known as Intermountain Health Care or more commonly IHC; it is now. Intermountain Healthcare is headquartered in Salt Lake City, Utah, and currently employs over 32,000 people.
Interprofessional education	Interprofessional education refers to occasions when students from two or more professions in health and social care learn together during all or part of their professional training with the object of cultivating collaborative practice for providing client- or patient-centered health care. Interprofessional learning involves students learning from students from other professions, as well as learning with students from other professions, for example in the classroom, and learning about other professions. Associated terms include 'multi-professional education', 'common learning', 'shared learning', and 'interdisciplinary learning.'

10. THE HEALTH WORKFORCE

Bundled payment	Bundled payment, also known as episode-based payment, episode payment, episode-of-care payment, case rate, evidence-based case rate, global bundled payment, global payment, package pricing, or packaged pricing, is defined as the reimbursement of health care providers (such as hospitals and physicians) 'on the basis of expected costs for clinically-defined episodes of care.' It has been described as 'a middle ground' between fee-for-service reimbursement (in which providers are paid for each service rendered to a patient) and capitation (in which providers are paid a 'lump sum' per patient regardless of how many services the patient receives). Bundled payments have been proposed in the health care reform debate in the United States as a strategy for reducing health care costs, especially during the Obama administration (2009-present). In the mid-1980s, it was believed that Medicare's then-new hospital prospective payment system using diagnosis-related groups may have led to hospitals' discharging patients to post-hospital care (e.g., skilled nursing facilities) more quickly than appropriate in order to save money.
Incentive	Since human beings are purposeful creatures, the study of incentive structures is central to the study of all economic activity (both in terms of individual decision-making and in terms of co-operation and competition within a larger institutional structure). Economic analysis, then, of the differences between societies (and between different organizations within a society) largely amounts to characterizing the differences in incentive structures faced by individuals involved in these collective efforts. Ultimately, incentives aim to provide value for money and contribute to organizational success.
Human services	Human services refers to a variety of delivery systems such as social welfare services, education, mental health services, and other forms of healthcare. Human services professionals may provide services directly to clients or help clients access services. Human services professionals also manage agencies that provide these services.
Service	In economics, a service is an intangible commodity. More specifically, services are an intangible equivalent of economic goods. Service provision is often an economic activity where the buyer does not generally, except by exclusive contract, obtain exclusive ownership of the thing purchased.
Electronic health record	An electronic health record is an evolving concept defined as a systematic collection of electronic health information about individual patients or populations. It is a record in digital format that is theoretically capable of being shared across different health care settings. In some cases this sharing can occur by way of network-connected enterprise-wide information systems and other information networks or exchanges.
Health record	The terms medical record, health record, and medical chart are used somewhat interchangeably to describe the systematic documentation of a single patient's medical history and care across time within one particular health care provider's jurisdiction.

	The medical record includes a variety of types of 'notes' entered over time by health care professionals, recording observations and administration of drugs and therapies, orders for the administration of drugs and therapies, test results, x-rays, reports, etc. The maintenance of complete and accurate medical records is a requirement of health care providers and is generally enforced as a licensing or certification prerequisite.
Information technology	Information Technology is the branch of engineering that deals with the use of computers and telecommunications to store, retrieve and transmit information.
Medi-Cal	The California Medical Assistance Program (Medi-Cal is the name of the California Medicaid welfare program serving low-income families, seniors, persons with disabilities, children in foster care, pregnant women, and certain low-income adults. It is jointly administered by the California Department of Health Care Services (DHCS) and the Centers for Medicare and Medicaid Services (CMS), with many services implemented at the local level mainly by the counties of California. Approximately 8.8 million citizens were enrolled in Medi-Cal for at least 1 month in 2009-10, or about 23% of California's population.
Medical home	The medical home, is a team based health care delivery model led by a physician that provides comprehensive and continuous medical care to patients with the goal of obtaining maximized health outcomes (American College of Physicians) (American Academy of Family Physicians). It is 'an approach to providing comprehensive primary care for children, youth and adults'. The provision of medical homes may allow better access to health care, increase satisfaction with care, and improve health.
Nurse Practitioner	A Nurse Practitioner is an Advanced Practice Nurse (APN) who has completed graduate-level education (either a Master's or a Doctoral degree). Additional APN roles include the Certified Registered Nurse Anesthetist (CRNA)s, CNMs, and CNSs. All Nurse Practitioners are Registered Nurses who have completed extensive additional education, training, and have a dramatically expanded scope of practice over the traditional RN role.
Patient-centered medical home	The medical home, also known as the patient-centered medical home is a team based health care delivery model led by a physician, P.A., or N.P. that provides comprehensive and continuous medical care to patients with the goal of obtaining maximized health outcomes (American College of Physicians) (American Academy of Family Physicians). It is 'an approach to providing comprehensive primary care for children, youth and adults'. The provision of medical homes may allow better access to health care, increase satisfaction with care, and improve health.
RECOrd	RECOrd is a Local Biological Records Centre (LRC) serving Cheshire, Halton, Warrington and Wirral (including the vice-county 'pan-handle' boundary around Stockport) - 'The Cheshire region'. It provides a local facility for the storage, validation and usage of Cheshire-based biological data under the National Biodiversity Network (NBN) project.

10. THE HEALTH WORKFORCE

	It is one of a number of local Biological Records Centres across Britain which together aim to give complete geographic coverage of the UK.
	The organisation is housed in Oakfield House at Chester Zoo.
Kaiser Permanente	Kaiser Permanente is an integrated managed care consortium, based in Oakland, California, United States, founded in 1945 by industrialist Henry J. Kaiser and physician Sidney Garfield. Kaiser Permanente is made up of three distinct groups of entities: the Kaiser Foundation Health Plan and its regional operating subsidiaries; Kaiser Foundation Hospitals; and the autonomous regional Permanente Medical Groups. As of 2006, Kaiser Permanente operates in nine states and the District of Columbia, and is the largest managed care organization in the United States.
Case study	A case study is an intensive analysis of an individual unit (e.g., a person, group, or event) stressing developmental factors in relation to context. The case study is common in social sciences and life sciences. Case studies may be descriptive or explanatory.

1. In economics, a _____ is an intangible commodity. More specifically, _____s are an intangible equivalent of economic goods.

    _____ provision is often an economic activity where the buyer does not generally, except by exclusive contract, obtain exclusive ownership of the thing purchased.

    a. Shipping list
    b. Stockout
    c. Service
    d. Supply chain

2. . The terms medical record, _____, and medical chart are used somewhat interchangeably to describe the systematic documentation of a single patient's medical history and care across time within one particular health care provider's jurisdiction. The medical record includes a variety of types of 'notes' entered over time by health care professionals, recording observations and administration of drugs and therapies, orders for the administration of drugs and therapies, test results, x-rays, reports, etc. The maintenance of complete and accurate medical records is a requirement of health care providers and is generally enforced as a licensing or certification prerequisite.

    a. 19NorDehydroepiandrosterone
    b. Enterprise master patient index

c. Health record

d. Immunization registry

3. _____ refers to a variety of delivery systems such as social welfare services, education, mental health services, and other forms of healthcare. _____ professionals may provide services directly to clients or help clients access services. _____ professionals also manage agencies that provide these services.

a. Human services

b. Patient Centered Outcomes

c. Promotoras

d. Stem cell treatments

4. The California Medical Assistance Program (_____ is the name of the California Medicaid welfare program serving low-income families, seniors, persons with disabilities, children in foster care, pregnant women, and certain low-income adults. It is jointly administered by the California Department of Health Care Services (DHCS) and the Centers for Medicare and Medicaid Services (CMS), with many services implemented at the local level mainly by the counties of California. Approximately 8.8 million citizens were enrolled in _____ for at least 1 month in 2009-10, or about 23% of California's population.

a. Medical billing

b. Medically Unlikely Edit

c. Medicare Advantage

d. Medi-Cal

5. A _____ is an Advanced Practice Nurse (APN) who has completed graduate-level education (either a Master's or a Doctoral degree). Additional APN roles include the Certified Registered Nurse Anesthetist (CRNA)s, CNMs, and CNSs. All _____s are Registered Nurses who have completed extensive additional education, training, and have a dramatically expanded scope of practice over the traditional RN role.

a. child health

b. Perioperative Nursing

c. disease prevention

d. Nurse Practitioner

1. c
2. c
3. a
4. d
5. d

You can take the complete Online Interactive Chapter Practice Test

for 10. THE HEALTH WORKFORCE
on all key terms, persons, places, and concepts.

No Additional Costs

http://www.Cram101.com

Register, send an email request to Travis.Reese@Cram101.com to get your user Id and password.

Include your customer order number, and ISBN number from your studyguide Retailer.

11. HEALTH CARE FINANCING

CHAPTER OUTLINE: KEY TERMS, PEOPLE, PLACES, CONCEPTS

Incentive

Extension

Health

Health insurance

Copayment

Gross domestic product

Fertility clinic

Service

Accreditation

Kaiser Permanente

Medicare

Public health

Charity care

Health insurance exchange

Balanced Budget

Balanced Budget Act

Medicaid

Managed care

Strategy

Department of Health and Human Services

Indian Health Service

CHAPTER OUTLINE: KEY TERMS, PEOPLE, PLACES, CONCEPTS

Health care

Workers' compensation

Consolidated Omnibus Budget Reconciliation Act

Income

Preferred provider organization

Service provider

Human services

Accountable care organization

Consumer driven health care

Diagnosis-related group

Resource-based relative value scale

Waterlow score

Integrated delivery system

Capitation

GLOBAL

Case study

11. HEALTH CARE FINANCING

Incentive	Since human beings are purposeful creatures, the study of incentive structures is central to the study of all economic activity (both in terms of individual decision-making and in terms of co-operation and competition within a larger institutional structure). Economic analysis, then, of the differences between societies (and between different organizations within a society) largely amounts to characterizing the differences in incentive structures faced by individuals involved in these collective efforts. Ultimately, incentives aim to provide value for money and contribute to organizational success.
Extension	Extension is a movement of a joint that results in increased angle between two bones or body surfaces at a joint. Extension usually results in straightening of the bones or body surfaces involved. For example, Extension is produced by extending the flexed (bent) elbow.
Health	Health is the level of functional or metabolic efficiency of a living being. In humans, it is the general condition of a person's mind and body, usually meaning to be free from illness, injury or pain (as in 'good health' or 'healthy'). The World Health Organization (WHO) defined health in its broader sense in 1946 as 'a state of complete physical, mental, and social well-being and not merely the absence of disease or infirmity.' Although this definition has been subject to controversy, in particular as lacking operational value and because of the problem created by use of the word 'complete', it remains the most enduring .
Health insurance	Health insurance is insurance against the risk of incurring medical expenses among individuals. By estimating the overall risk of health care and health system expenses among a targeted group, an insurer can develop a routine finance structure, such as a monthly premium or payroll tax, to ensure that money is available to pay for the health care benefits specified in the insurance agreement. The benefit is administered by a central organization such as a government agency, private business, or not-for-profit entity.
Copayment	In the United States, copayment is accessed. It is technically a form of coinsurance, but is defined differently in health insurance where a coinsurance is a percentage payment after the deductible up to a certain limit. It must be paid before any policy benefit is payable by an insurance company.
Gross domestic product	Gross domestic product is the market value of all officially recognized final goods and services produced within a country in a year, or other given period of time. gross domestic product per capita is often considered an indicator of a country's standard of living. gross domestic product per capita is not a measure of personal income .
Fertility clinic	Fertility clinics are staffed medical clinics that assist couples, and , who want to become parents but for medical reasons have been unable to achieve this goal via the natural course. Clinics apply a number of tests and sometimes very advanced medical procedures to obtain the desired conceptions and pregnancies.

Service	In economics, a service is an intangible commodity. More specifically, services are an intangible equivalent of economic goods. Service provision is often an economic activity where the buyer does not generally, except by exclusive contract, obtain exclusive ownership of the thing purchased.
Accreditation	Accreditation is a process in which certification of competency, authority, or credibility is presented. Organizations that issue credentials or certify third parties against official standards are themselves formally accredited by accreditation bodies (such as UKAS); hence they are sometimes known as 'accredited certification bodies'. The accreditation process ensures that their certification practices are acceptable, typically meaning that they are competent to test and certify third parties, behave ethically and employ suitable quality assurance.
Kaiser Permanente	Kaiser Permanente is an integrated managed care consortium, based in Oakland, California, United States, founded in 1945 by industrialist Henry J. Kaiser and physician Sidney Garfield. Kaiser Permanente is made up of three distinct groups of entities: the Kaiser Foundation Health Plan and its regional operating subsidiaries; Kaiser Foundation Hospitals; and the autonomous regional Permanente Medical Groups. As of 2006, Kaiser Permanente operates in nine states and the District of Columbia, and is the largest managed care organization in the United States.
Medicare	Medicare is the unofficial name for Canada's publicly funded universal health insurance system. The formal terminology for the insurance system is provided by the Canada Health Act and the health insurance legislation of the individual provinces and territories. Under the terms of the Canada Health Act, all 'insured persons' (basically, legal residents of Canada, including permanent residents) are entitled to receive 'insured services' without copayment.
Public health	Public health is 'the science and art of preventing disease, prolonging life and promoting health through the organized efforts and informed choices of society, organizations, public and private, communities and individuals' (1920, C.E.A. Winslow). It is concerned with threats to health based on population health analysis. The population in question can be as small as a handful of people or as large as all the inhabitants of several continents (for instance, in the case of a pandemic).
Charity care	In the United States, charity care is health care provided for free or at reduced prices to low income patients. The percentage of doctors providing charity care dropped from 76% in 1996-97 to 68% in 2004-2005. Potential reasons for the decline include changes in physician practice patterns and increasing financial pressures. In 2006, Senate investigators found that many hospitals did not inform patients that charity care was available.

11. HEALTH CARE FINANCING

Health insurance exchange	A health insurance exchange is a set of government-regulated and standardized health care plans in the United States, from which individuals may purchase health insurance eligible for federal subsidies. All exchanges must be fully certified and operational by January 1, 2014, under federal law. Acronym HIX (Health Insurance Exchange) is emerging as the de facto acronym across state and federal government stakeholders, and the private sector technology and service providers that are helping states build their exchanges.
Balanced Budget	A balanced budget is a budget with revenues equal to expenditures, and neither a budget deficit nor a budget surplus ('the accounts balance'). More generally, it refers to a budget with no deficit, but possibly with a surplus. A cyclically balanced budget is a budget that is not necessarily balanced year-to-year, but is balanced over the economic cycle, running a surplus in boom years and running a deficit in lean years, with these offsetting over time.
Balanced Budget Act	The Balanced Budget Act of 1997, (Pub.L. 105-33, 111 Stat. 251), was signed into law on August 5, 1997. It was an omnibus legislative package enacted using the budget reconciliation process and designed to balance the federal budget by 2002. Among many other things, the Act contained major Medicare reforms. .
Medicaid	Medicaid is the United States health program for families and individuals with low income and resources. It is a means-tested program that is jointly funded by the state and federal governments, and is managed by the states. People served by Medicaid are U.S. citizens or legal permanent residents, including low-income adults, their children, and people with certain disabilities.
Managed care	The term managed care is used in the United States to describe a variety of techniques intended to reduce the cost of providing health benefits and improve the quality of care ('managed care techniques') for organizations that use those techniques or provide them as services to other organizations ('managed care, or to describe systems of financing and delivering health care to enrollees organized around managed care techniques and concepts ('managed care delivery systems'). ...intended to reduce unnecessary health care costs through a variety of mechanisms, including: economic incentives for physicians and patients to select less costly forms of care; programs for reviewing the medical necessity of specific services; increased beneficiary cost sharing; controls on inpatient admissions and lengths of stay; the establishment of cost-sharing incentives for outpatient surgery; selective contracting with health care providers; and the intensive management of high-cost health care cases. The programs may be provided in a variety of settings, such as Health Maintenance Organizations and Preferred Provider Organizations.
Strategy	Strategy is a general, undetailed plan of action, encompassing a long period of time, to achieve a complicated goal.

Strategy, as a way of action, becomes necessary in a situation when, for the direct achievement of the main goal, the available resources are not enough. The task of strategy is an efficient use of the available resources for the achievement of the main goal.

Department of Health and Human Services	The United States Department of Health and Human Services (HHS) is a Cabinet department of the United States government with the goal of protecting the health of all Americans and providing essential human services. Its motto is 'Improving the health, safety, and well-being of America'. Before its education functions were spun off in 1979, it was called the Department of Health, Education, and Welfare.

· 1 History · 2 Agencies

· 2.1 Office of the Secretary (OS) · 2.2 Operating divisions · 3

· Immediate Office of the Secretary (IOS) - currently led by Kathleen Sebelius · Office of the Deputy Secretary (DS) - currently led by Deputy Secretary Bill Corr · Assistant Secretary for Administration and Management (ASAM)

· Program Support Center (PSC) - currently led by Director Philip Van Landingham · Assistant Secretary for Legislation (ASL) · Assistant Secretary for Planning and Evaluation (ASPE) · Assistant Secretary for Preparedness and Response (ASPR)

· Biomedical Advanced Research and Development Authority (BARDA)

· Project BioShield · Public Health Emergency Medical Countermeasures Enterprise (PHEMCE) · Assistant Secretary for Public Affairs (ASPA) · Assistant Secretary for Resources and Technology (ASRT) · Departmental Appeals Board (DAB) · Office for Civil Rights (OCR) · Office of Global Health Affairs (OGHA) · Office of Intergovernmental Affairs (IGA) · Office of the Secretary's Regional Directors · Office of the General Counsel (OGC) · Office of Inspector General (OIG) - currently led by Inspector General Daniel R. Levinson · Office of Medicare Hearings and Appeals (OMHA) · Office of the National Coordinator for Health Information Technology (ONC) · Public Health Service (PHS) / Office of the Assistant Secretary for Health (ASH) - currently led by Assistant Secretary, Howard K. Koh

· Office of Public Health and Science (OPHS) · Office of the Surgeon General - currently led by Acting Surgeon General, Rear Admiral Steven K. Galson

· U.S. Public Health Service (USPHS) Commissioned Corps · Office on Disability (OD - currently led by Director Henry Claypool · Center for Faith-Based and Community Initiatives (CFBCI) |

11. HEALTH CARE FINANCING

· Administration for Children and Families (ACF) - currently led by Principal Deputy Assistant Secretary David Hansell · Administration on Aging (AoA) - currently led by Assistant Secretary Kathy Greenlee · Agency for Healthcare Research and Quality (AHRQ) - currently led by Director Carolyn Clancy · Agency for Toxic Substances and Disease Registry (ATSDR) - currently led by Administrator Thomas R. Frieden · Centers for Disease Control and Prevention (CDC) - currently led by Director Thomas R. Frieden · Centers for Medicare and Medicaid Services (CMS)- currently led by Acting Administrator Charlene Frizzera · Food and Drug Administration (FDA) - currently led by Commissioner Margaret Hamburg · Health Resources and Services Administration (HRSA) - currently led by Administrator Mary Wakefield · Indian Health Service (IHS) - currently led by Acting Director, Robert G. McSwain · National Institutes of Health (NIH) - currently led by Director Francis Collins · Substance Abuse and Mental Health Services Administration (SAMHSA) - currently led by Administrator Charles Curie

(Several agencies within HHS are components of the Public Health Service (PHS), including AHRQ, ASPR, ATSDR, CDC, FDA, HRSA, IHS, NIH, SAMHSA, OGHA, and OPHS).

· Social Security Administration, made independent in 1995. · Health Care Financing Administration

The Department of Health and Human Services' budget includes more than 300 programs, covering a wide spectrum of activities. Some highlights include:

· Health and social science research · Preventing disease, including immunization services · Assuring food and drug safety · Medicare (health insurance for elderly and disabled Americans) and Medicaid (health insurance for low-income people) · Health information technology · Financial assistance and services for low-income families · Improving maternal and infant health, including a Nurse Home Visitation to support first-time mothers. · Head Start (pre-school education and services) · Faith-based and community initiatives · Preventing child abuse and domestic violence · Substance abuse treatment and prevention · Services for older Americans, including home-delivered meals · Comprehensive health services for Native Americans · Medical preparedness for emergencies, including potential terrorism.

Indian Health Service	The Indian Health Service is an operating division (OPDIV) within the U.S. Department of Health and Human Services (HHS). Indian Health Service is responsible for providing medical and public health services to members of federally recognized Tribes and Alaska Natives. Indian Health Service is the principal federal health care provider and health advocate for Indian people, and its goal is to raise their health status to the highest possible level.
Health care	Health care is the diagnosis, treatment, and prevention of disease, illness, injury, and other physical and mental impairments in humans. Health care is delivered by practitioners in medicine, chiropractic, dentistry, nursing, pharmacy, allied health, and other care providers. It refers to the work done in providing primary care, secondary care and tertiary care, as well as in public health.

Workers' compensation	Workers' compensation is a form of insurance that provides wage replacement and medical benefits for employees who are injured in the course of employment, in exchange for mandatory relinquishment of the employee's right to sue his or her employer for the tort of negligence. The tradeoff between assured, limited coverage and lack of recourse outside the worker compensation system is known as 'the compensation bargain.' While plans differ between jurisdictions, provision can be made for weekly payments in place of wages (functioning in this case as a form of disability insurance), compensation for economic loss (past and future), reimbursement or payment of medical and like expenses (functioning in this case as a form of health insurance), and benefits payable to the dependents of workers killed during employment (functioning in this case as a form of life insurance). General damages for pain and suffering, and punitive damages for employer negligence, are generally not available in worker compensation plans, and negligence is generally not an issue in the case.
Consolidated Omnibus Budget Reconciliation Act	The Consolidated Omnibus Budget Reconciliation Act of 1985, is a law passed by the U.S. Congress and signed by President Reagan that, among other things, mandates an insurance program giving some employees the ability to continue health insurance coverage after leaving employment. Consolidated Omnibus Budget Reconciliation Act includes amendments to the Employee Retirement Income Security Act of 1974 (ERISA). The law deals with a great variety of subjects, such as tobacco price supports, railroads, private pension plans, disability insurance, and the postal service , but it is perhaps best known for Title X, which amends the Internal Revenue Code and the Public Health Service Act to deny income tax deductions to employers for contributions to a group health plan unless such plan meets certain continuing coverage requirements.
Income	Income is the consumption and savings opportunity gained by an entity within a specified timeframe, which is generally expressed in monetary terms. However, for households and individuals, 'income is the sum of all the wages, salaries, profits, interests payments, rents and other forms of earnings received... in a given period of time.' In the field of public economics, the term may refer to the accumulation of both monetary and non-monetary consumption ability, with the former (monetary) being used as a proxy for total income. Increase in income Income per capita has been increasing steadily in almost every country.
Preferred provider organization	In health insurance in the United States, a preferred provider organization is a managed care organization of medical doctors, hospitals, and other health care providers who have covenanted with an insurer or a third-party administrator to provide health care at reduced rates to the insurer's or administrator's clients. Overview A preferred provider organization is a subscription-based medical care arrangement.

11. HEALTH CARE FINANCING

Service provider	A service provider is a company that provides organizations with consulting, legal, real estate, education, communications, storage, processing, and many other services. Although the term service provider can refer to organizational sub-units, it is more generally used to refer to third party or outsourced suppliers, including telecommunications service providers (TSPs), application service providers (ASPs), storage service providers (SSPs), and Internet service providers (ISPs).
	IT professionals sometimes differentiate between service providers by categorizing them as type I, II, or III. The three service types are recognized by the IT industry although specifically defined by ITIL and the US Telecommunications Act of 1996•Type I: internal service provider•Type II: shared service provider•Type III: external service provider
	don't ever Type III SPs provide IT services to external customers and subsequently can be referred to as external service providers (ESPs) which range from a full IT organization/service outsource via managed services or MSPs (managed service providers) to limited product feature delivery via ASPs (application service providers).
Human services	Human services refers to a variety of delivery systems such as social welfare services, education, mental health services, and other forms of healthcare. Human services professionals may provide services directly to clients or help clients access services. Human services professionals also manage agencies that provide these services.
Accountable care organization	An accountable care organization is a healthcare organization characterized by a payment and care delivery model that seeks to tie provider reimbursements to quality metrics and reductions in the total cost of care for an assigned population of patients. A group of coordinated health care providers forms an Accountable care organization, which then provides care to a group of patients. The Accountable care organization may use a range of payment models (capitation, fee-for-service with asymmetric or symmetric shared savings, etc)..
Consumer driven health care	Defined narrowly, consumer driven health care refers to health insurance plans that allow members to use personal Health Savings Accounts (HSAs), Health Reimbursement Arrangements (HRAs) while a high-deductible health insurance policy protects them from catastrophic medical expenses. High-deductible policies cost less, but the user pays routine medical claims using a pre-funded spending account, often with a special debit card provided by a bank or insurance plan. If the balance on this account runs out, the user then pays claims just like under a regular deductible.
Diagnosis-related group	Diagnosis-related group is a system to classify hospital cases into one of originally 467 groups. The 467th group was 'Ungroupable'. This system of classification was developed as a collaborative project by Robert B Fetter, PhD, of the Yale School of Management, and John D Thompson, MPH, of the Yale School of Public Health.
Resource-based relative value scale	Resource-based relative value scale is a schema used to determine how much money medical providers should be paid.

	It is partially used by Medicare in the United States and by nearly all Health maintenance organizations (HMOs). Resource based relative value scale assigns procedures performed by a physician or other medical provider a relative value which is adjusted by geographic region (so a procedure performed in Manhattan is worth more than a procedure performed in Dallas).
Waterlow score	The 'Waterlow score gives an estimated risk of a patient developing a pressure sore. It is named after Judy Waterlow.
Integrated delivery system	An integrated delivery system is a network of health care organizations under a parent holding company. Some Integrated delivery system have an HMO component, while others are a network of physicians only, or of physicians and hospitals. Thus, the term is used broadly to define an organization that provides a continuum of health care services.
Capitation	Capitation is a method of paying health care service providers (e.g., physicians or nurse practitioners) a set amount for each enrolled person assigned to that physician or group of physicians, whether or not that person seeks care, per period of time. Generally these providers are contracted with a type of health maintenance organization (HMO) known as an independent practice association . The HMO contracts with the providers to have the latter take care of patients enrolled in the HMO. Most often, payment for such a service is under the capitation system.
GLOBAL	GLOBAL was a language developed in industry and sold off privately as an expert system. It was used to design several biopharmaceutical products, and sold to Tularik (Amgen). Prometheus used for drug system design was written using GLOBAL and is described on this Cray software specification.
Case study	A case study is an intensive analysis of an individual unit (e.g., a person, group, or event) stressing developmental factors in relation to context. The case study is common in social sciences and life sciences. Case studies may be descriptive or explanatory.

11. HEALTH CARE FINANCING

1. _____s are staffed medical clinics that assist couples, and , who want to become parents but for medical reasons have been unable to achieve this goal via the natural course. Clinics apply a number of tests and sometimes very advanced medical procedures to obtain the desired conceptions and pregnancies.

   For the male, semen collection is a standard diagnostic test to ascertain problems with the semen quality.

   a. Fertility clinic
   b. Drawer test
   c. Transmyocardial laser revascularization
   d. Loop electrosurgical excision procedure

2. _____ was a language developed in industry and sold off privately as an expert system. It was used to design several biopharmaceutical products, and sold to Tularik (Amgen).

   Prometheus used for drug system design was written using _____ and is described on this Cray software specification.

   a. High-content screening
   b. High-throughput screening
   c. History of pharmacy
   d. GLOBAL

3. The _____ is an operating division (OPDIV) within the U.S. Department of Health and Human Services (HHS). _____ is responsible for providing medical and public health services to members of federally recognized Tribes and Alaska Natives. _____ is the principal federal health care provider and health advocate for Indian people, and its goal is to raise their health status to the highest possible level.

   a. Indian Health Service
   b. UMass Memorial Health Care
   c. UNC Health Care
   d. University of Chicago Medical Center

4. _____ refers to a variety of delivery systems such as social welfare services, education, mental health services, and other forms of healthcare. _____ professionals may provide services directly to clients or help clients access services. _____ professionals also manage agencies that provide these services.

   a. Maxim Healthcare Services
   b. Patient Centered Outcomes
   c. Human services
   d. Stem cell treatments

5. . _____ is the market value of all officially recognized final goods and services produced within a country in a year, or other given period of time. _____ per capita is often considered an indicator of a country's standard of living.

_____ per capita is not a measure of personal income .

a. 19NorDehydroepiandrosterone
b. Cost-shifting
c. Gross domestic product
d. Deductible

1. a
2. d
3. a
4. c
5. c

You can take the complete Online Interactive Chapter Practice Test

for 11. HEALTH CARE FINANCING
on all key terms, persons, places, and concepts.

No Additional Costs

http://www.Cram101.com

Register, send an email request to Travis.Reese@Cram101.com to get your user Id and password.

Include your customer order number, and ISBN number from your studyguide Retailer.

12. HEALTH CARE COSTS AND VALUE

CHAPTER OUTLINE: KEY TERMS, PEOPLE, PLACES, CONCEPTS

	Gross domestic product
	Health
	Health care
	Revenue
	Tax revenue
	Income
	Medicare
	Service
	Defensive medicine
	Fee-for-service
	End-of-life care
	Copayment
	Control
	Malpractice
	Medi-Cal
	Medical malpractice
	Human services
	Electronic medical record
	Medical record
	Procedures
	RECOrd

12. HEALTH CARE COSTS AND VALUE

CHAPTER OUTLINE: KEY TERMS, PEOPLE, PLACES, CONCEPTS

	Cost reduction
	Purchasing
	Value-based
	Kaiser Permanente
	Case study

CHAPTER HIGHLIGHTS & NOTES: KEY TERMS, PEOPLE, PLACES, CONCEPTS

Gross domestic product	Gross domestic product is the market value of all officially recognized final goods and services produced within a country in a year, or other given period of time. gross domestic product per capita is often considered an indicator of a country's standard of living. gross domestic product per capita is not a measure of personal income .
Health	Health is the level of functional or metabolic efficiency of a living being. In humans, it is the general condition of a person's mind and body, usually meaning to be free from illness, injury or pain (as in 'good health' or 'healthy'). The World Health Organization (WHO) defined health in its broader sense in 1946 as 'a state of complete physical, mental, and social well-being and not merely the absence of disease or infirmity.' Although this definition has been subject to controversy, in particular as lacking operational value and because of the problem created by use of the word 'complete', it remains the most enduring .
Health care	Health care is the diagnosis, treatment, and prevention of disease, illness, injury, and other physical and mental impairments in humans. Health care is delivered by practitioners in medicine, chiropractic, dentistry, nursing, pharmacy, allied health, and other care providers. It refers to the work done in providing primary care, secondary care and tertiary care, as well as in public health.
Revenue	In business, revenue is income that a company receives from its normal business activities, usually from the sale of goods and services to customers. In many countries, such as the United Kingdom, revenue is referred to as turnover. Some companies receive revenue from interest, dividends or royalties paid to them by other companies.
Tax revenue	Tax revenue is the income that is gained by governments through taxation.

Just as there are different types of tax, the form in which tax revenue is collected also differs; furthermore, the agency that collects the tax may not be part of central government, but may be an alternative third-party licenced to collect tax which they themselves will use. For example:•In the UK, the DVLA collects vehicle excise duty, which is then passed onto the treasury

Tax revenues on purchases can come from two forms: 'tax' itself is a percentage of the price added to the purchase (such as sales tax in US states, or VAT in the UK), while 'duty' is a fixed amount added to the purchase price (such as is commonly found on cigarettes).

Income	Income is the consumption and savings opportunity gained by an entity within a specified timeframe, which is generally expressed in monetary terms. However, for households and individuals, 'income is the sum of all the wages, salaries, profits, interests payments, rents and other forms of earnings received... in a given period of time.'
	In the field of public economics, the term may refer to the accumulation of both monetary and non-monetary consumption ability, with the former (monetary) being used as a proxy for total income. Increase in income
	Income per capita has been increasing steadily in almost every country.
Medicare	Medicare is the unofficial name for Canada's publicly funded universal health insurance system. The formal terminology for the insurance system is provided by the Canada Health Act and the health insurance legislation of the individual provinces and territories.
	Under the terms of the Canada Health Act, all 'insured persons' (basically, legal residents of Canada, including permanent residents) are entitled to receive 'insured services' without copayment.
Service	In economics, a service is an intangible commodity. More specifically, services are an intangible equivalent of economic goods.
	Service provision is often an economic activity where the buyer does not generally, except by exclusive contract, obtain exclusive ownership of the thing purchased.
Defensive medicine	Defensive medicine is the practice of diagnostic or therapeutic measures conducted primarily not to ensure the health of the patient, but as a safeguard against possible malpractice liability. Fear of litigation has been cited as the driving force behind defensive medicine, however even critics of the litigation system have found that a more fundamental motive may be a deliberate increase of services to create revenue.

12. HEALTH CARE COSTS AND VALUE

Fee-for-service	Fee-for-service is a payment model where services are unbundled and paid for separately. In health care, it gives an incentive for physicians to provide more treatments because payment is dependent on the quantity of care, rather than quality of care. Similarly, when patients are shielded from paying (cost-sharing) by health insurance coverage, they are incentivized to welcome any medical service that might do some good.
End-of-life care	In medicine, end-of-life care refers to medical care not only of patients in the final hours or days of their lives, but more broadly, medical care of all those with a terminal illness or terminal condition that has become advanced, progressive and incurable. Regarding cancer care the United States National Cancer Institute writes: When a patient's health care team determines that the cancer can no longer be controlled, medical testing and cancer treatment often stop. But the patient's care continues.
Copayment	In the United States, copayment is accessed. It is technically a form of coinsurance, but is defined differently in health insurance where a coinsurance is a percentage payment after the deductible up to a certain limit. It must be paid before any policy benefit is payable by an insurance company.
Control	Controlling is ones of the managerial functions like planning, organizing, staffing and directing. It is an important function because it helps to check the errors and to take the corrective action so that deviation from standards are minimized and stated goals of the organization are achieved in desired manner.According to modern concepts, control is a foreseeing action whereas earlier concept of control was used only when errors were detected. Control in management means setting standards, measuring actual performance and taking corrective action.
Malpractice	In law, malpractice is a type of negligence in, which the professional under a duty to act, fails to follow generally accepted professional standards, and that breach of duty is the proximate cause of injury to a plaintiff who suffers harm. It is committed by a professional or her/his subordinates or agents on behalf of a client or patient that causes damages to the client or patient.
Medi-Cal	The California Medical Assistance Program (Medi-Cal is the name of the California Medicaid welfare program serving low-income families, seniors, persons with disabilities, children in foster care, pregnant women, and certain low-income adults. It is jointly administered by the California Department of Health Care Services (DHCS) and the Centers for Medicare and Medicaid Services (CMS), with many services implemented at the local level mainly by the counties of California. Approximately 8.8 million citizens were enrolled in Medi-Cal for at least 1 month in 2009-10, or about 23% of California's population.
Medical malpractice	Medical malpractice is professional negligence by act or omission by a health care provider in which the treatment provided falls below the accepted standard of practice in the medical community and causes injury or death to the patient, with most cases involving medical error.

	Standards and regulations for medical malpractice vary by country and jurisdiction within countries. Medical professionals may obtain professional liability insurances to offset the risk and costs of lawsuits based on medical malpractice.
Human services	Human services refers to a variety of delivery systems such as social welfare services, education, mental health services, and other forms of healthcare. Human services professionals may provide services directly to clients or help clients access services. Human services professionals also manage agencies that provide these services.
Electronic medical record	An electronic medical record is a computerized medical record created in an organization that delivers care, such as a hospital or physician's office. Electronic medical records tend to be a part of a local stand-alone health information system that allows storage, retrieval and modification of records. Comparison with paper-based records

Paper-based records are still by far the most common method of recording patient information for most hospitals and practices in the U.S. The majority of doctors still find their ease of data entry and low cost hard to part with. |
| Medical record | The terms medical record, health record, and medical chart are used somewhat interchangeably to describe the systematic documentation of a single patient's medical history and care across time within one particular health care provider's jurisdiction. The medical record includes a variety of types of 'notes' entered over time by health care professionals, recording observations and administration of drugs and therapies, orders for the administration of drugs and therapies, test results, x-rays, reports, etc. The maintenance of complete and accurate medical records is a requirement of health care providers and is generally enforced as a licensing or certification prerequisite. |
| Procedures | An ASC is a health care facility that specializes in providing surgery, including certain pain management and diagnostic (e.g., colonoscopy) services in an outpatient setting. Overall, the services provided can be generally called procedures In simple terms, ASC-qualified procedures can be considered procedures that are more intensive than those done in the average doctor's office but not so intensive as to require a hospital stay. |
| RECOrd | RECOrd is a Local Biological Records Centre (LRC) serving Cheshire, Halton, Warrington and Wirral (including the vice-county 'pan-handle' boundary around Stockport) - 'The Cheshire region'. It provides a local facility for the storage, validation and usage of Cheshire-based biological data under the National Biodiversity Network (NBN) project. It is one of a number of local Biological Records Centres across Britain which together aim to give complete geographic coverage of the UK.

The organisation is housed in Oakfield House at Chester Zoo. |

12. HEALTH CARE COSTS AND VALUE

Cost reduction	Cost reduction is the process used by companies to reduce their costs and increase their profits. Depending on a company's services or Product, the strategies can vary. Every decision in the product development process affects cost.
Purchasing	Purchasing refers to a business or organization attempting for acquiring goods or services to accomplish the goals of the enterprise. Though there are several organizations that attempt to set standards in the purchasing process, processes can vary greatly between organizations. Typically the word 'purchasing' is not used interchangeably with the word 'procurement', since procurement typically includes Expediting, Supplier Quality, and Traffic and Logistics (T&L) in addition to Purchasing.
Value-based	Value-based pricing is a pricing strategy which sets prices primarily, but not exclusively, on the value, perceived or estimated, to the customer rather than on the cost of the product or historical prices. Where is it successfully used, it will improve profitability due to the higher prices without impacting greatly on sales volumes. The approach is most successful when products are sold based on emotions (fashion), in niche markets, in shortages (e.g. drinks at open air festival at a hot summer day) or for indispensable add-ons (e.g. printer cartridges, headsets for cell phones).
Kaiser Permanente	Kaiser Permanente is an integrated managed care consortium, based in Oakland, California, United States, founded in 1945 by industrialist Henry J. Kaiser and physician Sidney Garfield. Kaiser Permanente is made up of three distinct groups of entities: the Kaiser Foundation Health Plan and its regional operating subsidiaries; Kaiser Foundation Hospitals; and the autonomous regional Permanente Medical Groups. As of 2006, Kaiser Permanente operates in nine states and the District of Columbia, and is the largest managed care organization in the United States.
Case study	A case study is an intensive analysis of an individual unit (e.g., a person, group, or event) stressing developmental factors in relation to context. The case study is common in social sciences and life sciences. Case studies may be descriptive or explanatory.

1. An ASC is a health care facility that specializes in providing surgery, including certain pain management and diagnostic (e.g., colonoscopy) services in an outpatient setting. Overall, the services provided can be generally called _____ In simple terms, ASC-qualified _____ can be considered _____ that are more intensive than those done in the average doctor's office but not so intensive as to require a hospital stay.

    a. Convenient care clinics
    b. Clinic
    c. Procedures
    d. Process analysis

2. _____ is the unofficial name for Canada's publicly funded universal health insurance system. The formal terminology for the insurance system is provided by the Canada Health Act and the health insurance legislation of the individual provinces and territories.

    Under the terms of the Canada Health Act, all 'insured persons' (basically, legal residents of Canada, including permanent residents) are entitled to receive 'insured services' without copayment.

    a. Medicare
    b. Public health system in India
    c. Robert Koch Institute
    d. Socialized medicine

3. _____ is the market value of all officially recognized final goods and services produced within a country in a year, or other given period of time. _____ per capita is often considered an indicator of a country's standard of living.

    _____ per capita is not a measure of personal income .

    a. 19NorDehydroepiandrosterone
    b. 2 mile
    c. 21-Hydroxylase
    d. Gross domestic product

4. . _____ is the income that is gained by governments through taxation.

    Just as there are different types of tax, the form in which _____ is collected also differs; furthermore, the agency that collects the tax may not be part of central government, but may be an alternative third-party licenced to collect tax which they themselves will use. For example:•In the UK, the DVLA collects vehicle excise duty, which is then passed onto the treasury

    _____s on purchases can come from two forms: 'tax' itself is a percentage of the price added to the purchase (such as sales tax in US states, or VAT in the UK), while 'duty' is a fixed amount added to the purchase price (such as is commonly found on cigarettes).

    a. Taxpayer

b. Taxpayer receipt

c. Value capture

d. Tax revenue

5. In business, _____ is income that a company receives from its normal business activities, usually from the sale of goods and services to customers. In many countries, such as the United Kingdom, _____ is referred to as turnover. Some companies receive _____ from interest, dividends or royalties paid to them by other companies.

a. RevPAR

b. Robinson Crusoe economy

c. Schedule delay

d. Revenue

ANSWER KEY
12. HEALTH CARE COSTS AND VALUE

1. c
2. a
3. d
4. d
5. d

You can take the complete Online Interactive Chapter Practice Test

for 12. HEALTH CARE COSTS AND VALUE
on all key terms, persons, places, and concepts.

No Additional Costs

http://www.Cram101.com

Register, send an email request to Travis.Reese@Cram101.com to get your user Id and password.

Include your customer order number, and ISBN number from your studyguide Retailer.

13. HIGH-QUALITY HEALTH CARE

CHAPTER OUTLINE: KEY TERMS, PEOPLE, PLACES, CONCEPTS

_____	Outcome
_____	Quality improvement
_____	Health
_____	Gross domestic product
_____	Infection
_____	Process
_____	Service
_____	Consolidated Omnibus Budget Reconciliation Act
_____	Department of Health and Human Services
_____	MONAHRQ
_____	Consumer
_____	Health care
_____	Initiative
_____	Medicare
_____	Purchasing
_____	Value-based
_____	Consumerism
_____	Accreditation
_____	Patient Protection and Affordable Care Act
_____	Joint Commission
_____	National Committee for Quality Assurance

13. HIGH-QUALITY HEALTH CARE

	Quality improvement organizations
	Intermountain Healthcare
	Case study

Outcome	In game theory, an outcome is a set of moves or strategies taken by the players, or it is their payoffs resulting from the actions or strategies taken by all players. The two are complementary in that, given knowledge of the set of strategies of all players, the final state of the game is known, as are any relevant payoffs. In a game where chance or a random event is involved, the outcome is not known from only the set of strategies, but is only realized when the random event(s) are realized.
Quality improvement	The term quality management has a specific meaning within many business sectors. This specific definition, which does not aim to assure 'good quality' by the more general definition, but rather to ensure that an organization or product is consistent, can be considered to have four main components: quality planning, quality control, quality assurance and quality improvement. Quality management is focused not only on product/service quality, but also the means to achieve it.
Health	Health is the level of functional or metabolic efficiency of a living being. In humans, it is the general condition of a person's mind and body, usually meaning to be free from illness, injury or pain (as in 'good health' or 'healthy'). The World Health Organization (WHO) defined health in its broader sense in 1946 as 'a state of complete physical, mental, and social well-being and not merely the absence of disease or infirmity.' Although this definition has been subject to controversy, in particular as lacking operational value and because of the problem created by use of the word 'complete', it remains the most enduring .
Gross domestic product	Gross domestic product is the market value of all officially recognized final goods and services produced within a country in a year, or other given period of time. gross domestic product per capita is often considered an indicator of a country's standard of living. gross domestic product per capita is not a measure of personal income .
Infection	An infection is the invasion of body tissues by disease-causing microorganisms, their multiplication and the reaction of body tissues to these microorganisms and the toxins that they produce.

	Infections are caused by microorganisms such as viruses, prions, bacteria, and viroids, though larger organisms like macroparasites and fungi can also infect.
	Hosts normally fight infections themselves via their immune system.
Process	In engineering a process is a set of interrelated tasks that, together, transform inputs into outputs. These tasks may be carried out by people, nature, or machines using resources; so an engineering process must be considered in the context of the agents carrying out the tasks, and the resource attributes involved. Systems Engineering normative documents and those related to Maturity Models are typically based on processes.
Service	In economics, a service is an intangible commodity. More specifically, services are an intangible equivalent of economic goods.
	Service provision is often an economic activity where the buyer does not generally, except by exclusive contract, obtain exclusive ownership of the thing purchased.
Consolidated Omnibus Budget Reconciliation Act	The Consolidated Omnibus Budget Reconciliation Act of 1985, is a law passed by the U.S. Congress and signed by President Reagan that, among other things, mandates an insurance program giving some employees the ability to continue health insurance coverage after leaving employment. Consolidated Omnibus Budget Reconciliation Act includes amendments to the Employee Retirement Income Security Act of 1974 (ERISA). The law deals with a great variety of subjects, such as tobacco price supports, railroads, private pension plans, disability insurance, and the postal service , but it is perhaps best known for Title X, which amends the Internal Revenue Code and the Public Health Service Act to deny income tax deductions to employers for contributions to a group health plan unless such plan meets certain continuing coverage requirements.
Department of Health and Human Services	The United States Department of Health and Human Services (HHS) is a Cabinet department of the United States government with the goal of protecting the health of all Americans and providing essential human services. Its motto is 'Improving the health, safety, and well-being of America'. Before its education functions were spun off in 1979, it was called the Department of Health, Education, and Welfare.
	· 1 History · 2 Agencies
	· 2.1 Office of the Secretary (OS) · 2.2 Operating divisions · 3
	· Immediate Office of the Secretary (IOS) - currently led by Kathleen Sebelius · Office of the Deputy Secretary (DS) - currently led by Deputy Secretary Bill Corr · Assistant Secretary for Administration and Management (ASAM)

13. HIGH-QUALITY HEALTH CARE

· Program Support Center (PSC) - currently led by Director Philip Van Landingham · Assistant Secretary for Legislation (ASL) · Assistant Secretary for Planning and Evaluation (ASPE) · Assistant Secretary for Preparedness and Response (ASPR)

· Biomedical Advanced Research and Development Authority (BARDA)

· Project BioShield · Public Health Emergency Medical Countermeasures Enterprise (PHEMCE) · Assistant Secretary for Public Affairs (ASPA) · Assistant Secretary for Resources and Technology (ASRT) · Departmental Appeals Board (DAB) · Office for Civil Rights (OCR) · Office of Global Health Affairs (OGHA) · Office of Intergovernmental Affairs (IGA) · Office of the Secretary's Regional Directors · Office of the General Counsel (OGC) · Office of Inspector General (OIG) - currently led by Inspector General Daniel R. Levinson · Office of Medicare Hearings and Appeals (OMHA) · Office of the National Coordinator for Health Information Technology (ONC) · Public Health Service (PHS) / Office of the Assistant Secretary for Health (ASH) - currently led by Assistant Secretary, Howard K. Koh

· Office of Public Health and Science (OPHS) · Office of the Surgeon General - currently led by Acting Surgeon General, Rear Admiral Steven K. Galson

· U.S. Public Health Service (USPHS) Commissioned Corps · Office on Disability (OD - currently led by Director Henry Claypool · Center for Faith-Based and Community Initiatives (CFBCI)

· Administration for Children and Families (ACF) - currently led by Principal Deputy Assistant Secretary David Hansell · Administration on Aging (AoA) - currently led by Assistant Secretary Kathy Greenlee · Agency for Healthcare Research and Quality (AHRQ) - currently led by Director Carolyn Clancy · Agency for Toxic Substances and Disease Registry (ATSDR) - currently led by Administrator Thomas R. Frieden · Centers for Disease Control and Prevention (CDC) - currently led by Director Thomas R. Frieden · Centers for Medicare and Medicaid Services (CMS)- currently led by Acting Administrator Charlene Frizzera · Food and Drug Administration (FDA) - currently led by Commissioner Margaret Hamburg · Health Resources and Services Administration (HRSA) - currently led by Administrator Mary Wakefield · Indian Health Service (IHS) - currently led by Acting Director, Robert G. McSwain · National Institutes of Health (NIH) - currently led by Director Francis Collins · Substance Abuse and Mental Health Services Administration (SAMHSA) - currently led by Administrator Charles Curie

(Several agencies within HHS are components of the Public Health Service (PHS), including AHRQ, ASPR, ATSDR, CDC, FDA, HRSA, IHS, NIH, SAMHSA, OGHA, and OPHS).

· Social Security Administration, made independent in 1995. · Health Care Financing Administration

The Department of Health and Human Services' budget includes more than 300 programs, covering a wide spectrum of activities. Some highlights include:

	· Health and social science research · Preventing disease, including immunization services · Assuring food and drug safety · Medicare (health insurance for elderly and disabled Americans) and Medicaid (health insurance for low-income people) · Health information technology · Financial assistance and services for low-income families · Improving maternal and infant health, including a Nurse Home Visitation to support first-time mothers. · Head Start (pre-school education and services) · Faith-based and community initiatives · Preventing child abuse and domestic violence · Substance abuse treatment and prevention · Services for older Americans, including home-delivered meals · Comprehensive health services for Native Americans · Medical preparedness for emergencies, including potential terrorism.
MONAHRQ	My Own Network, Powered by AHRQ (MONAHRQ) is a healthcare software product that enables an organization to input its own hospital administrative data and generate an interactive, data-driven querying website. It is a product of the Agency for Healthcare Research and Quality (AHRQ), part of the United States Department of Health and Human Services (DHHS). Overview and Purpose MONAHRQ - My Own Network, Powered by AHRQ - is a free, downloadable software product that helps organizations quickly and easily generate a health care reporting website suitable for the public, providers, or policymakers.
Consumer	Consumers are organisms of an ecological food chain that receive their energy by consuming other organisms. These organisms are formally referred to as heterotrophs, which includes animals, bacteria and fungus. Such organisms may consume by various means, including predation, parasitization, and biodegradation.
Health care	Health care is the diagnosis, treatment, and prevention of disease, illness, injury, and other physical and mental impairments in humans. Health care is delivered by practitioners in medicine, chiropractic, dentistry, nursing, pharmacy, allied health, and other care providers. It refers to the work done in providing primary care, secondary care and tertiary care, as well as in public health.
Initiative	An initiative represents an enterprise's readiness to embark on a new venture. Generally speaking, the motivation for an initiative arises from a desire to accomplish something that would benefit the enterprise, such as improving productivity, reducing costs or increasing market share. A typical initiative is expressed as a process and includes metrics and time frames.
Medicare	Medicare is the unofficial name for Canada's publicly funded universal health insurance system. The formal terminology for the insurance system is provided by the Canada Health Act and the health insurance legislation of the individual provinces and territories.

13. HIGH-QUALITY HEALTH CARE

Purchasing	Purchasing refers to a business or organization attempting for acquiring goods or services to accomplish the goals of the enterprise. Though there are several organizations that attempt to set standards in the purchasing process, processes can vary greatly between organizations. Typically the word 'purchasing' is not used interchangeably with the word 'procurement', since procurement typically includes Expediting, Supplier Quality, and Traffic and Logistics (T&L) in addition to Purchasing.
Value-based	Value-based pricing is a pricing strategy which sets prices primarily, but not exclusively, on the value, perceived or estimated, to the customer rather than on the cost of the product or historical prices. Where is it successfully used, it will improve profitability due to the higher prices without impacting greatly on sales volumes. The approach is most successful when products are sold based on emotions (fashion), in niche markets, in shortages (e.g. drinks at open air festival at a hot summer day) or for indispensable add-ons (e.g. printer cartridges, headsets for cell phones).
Consumerism	Consumerism is a social and economic order that encourages the purchase of goods and services in ever-greater amounts. Early criticisms of consumerism are present in the works of Thorstein Veblen (1899). Veblen's subject of examination, the newly emergent middle class arising at the turn of the twentieth century, comes to fruition by the end of the twentieth century through the process of globalization.
Accreditation	Accreditation is a process in which certification of competency, authority, or credibility is presented. Organizations that issue credentials or certify third parties against official standards are themselves formally accredited by accreditation bodies (such as UKAS); hence they are sometimes known as 'accredited certification bodies'. The accreditation process ensures that their certification practices are acceptable, typically meaning that they are competent to test and certify third parties, behave ethically and employ suitable quality assurance.
Patient Protection and Affordable Care Act	The Patient Protection and Affordable Care Act informally referred to as Obamacare, is a United States federal statute signed into law by President Barack Obama on March 23, 2010. The law (along with the Health Care and Education Reconciliation Act of 2010) is the principal health care reform legislation of the 111th United States Congress. PPACA requires individuals not covered by employer- or government-sponsored insurance plans to maintain minimal essential health insurance coverage or pay a penalty unless exempted for religious beliefs or financial hardship, a provision commonly referred to as the 'individual mandate'. The Act also reforms certain aspects of the private health insurance industry and public health insurance programs, increases insurance coverage of pre-existing conditions, expands access to insurance to 30 million Americans, and increases projected national medical spending while lowering projected Medicare spending.

Joint Commission	The Joint Commission formerly the Joint Commission on Accreditation of Healthcare Organizations (JCAHO) and previous to that the Joint Commission on Accreditation of Hospitals (JCAH), is a United States-based nonprofit organization that accredits more than 19,000 health care organizations and programs in the United States. A majority of state governments have come to recognize Joint Commission accreditation as a condition of licensure and the receipt of Medicaid reimbursement. Surveys (inspections) typically follow a triennial cycle, with findings made available to the public in an accreditation quality report on the Quality Check Web site.
National Committee for Quality Assurance	The National Committee for Quality Assurance is an independent 501(c)(3) non-profit organization in the United States designed to improve health care quality. It was established in 1990 with support from the Robert Wood Johnson Foundation. NCQA manages voluntary accreditation programs for individual physicians, health plans, and medical groups.
Quality improvement organizations	Quality Improvement Organizations monitor the appropriateness, effectiveness, and quality of care provided to Medicare beneficiaries. They are private contractor extensions of the federal government that work under the auspices of the U.S. Centers for Medicare and Medicaid Services (CMS). In recent years Quality improvement organizationss have undertaken to facilitate continual improvement of health care services within their constituent communities in addition to their original and ongoing statutory audit/inspection role of medical peer review, i.e., akin to the traditional function of quality assurance.
Intermountain Healthcare	Intermountain Health Care, Inc., officially doing business as as Intermountain Healthcare, is a non-profit healthcare system and is the largest healthcare provider in the Intermountain West. Until 2005 it known as Intermountain Health Care or more commonly IHC; it is now. Intermountain Healthcare is headquartered in Salt Lake City, Utah, and currently employs over 32,000 people.
Case study	A case study is an intensive analysis of an individual unit (e.g., a person, group, or event) stressing developmental factors in relation to context. The case study is common in social sciences and life sciences. Case studies may be descriptive or explanatory.

13. HIGH-QUALITY HEALTH CARE

1. In game theory, an _____ is a set of moves or strategies taken by the players, or it is their payoffs resulting from the actions or strategies taken by all players. The two are complementary in that, given knowledge of the set of strategies of all players, the final state of the game is known, as are any relevant payoffs. In a game where chance or a random event is involved, the _____ is not known from only the set of strategies, but is only realized when the random event(s) are realized.

   a. Ultimatum game
   b. Outcome
   c. Uncorrelated asymmetry
   d. Uniform price auction

2. _____ is a process in which certification of competency, authority, or credibility is presented.

   Organizations that issue credentials or certify third parties against official standards are themselves formally accredited by _____ bodies (such as UKAS); hence they are sometimes known as 'accredited certification bodies'. The _____ process ensures that their certification practices are acceptable, typically meaning that they are competent to test and certify third parties, behave ethically and employ suitable quality assurance.

   a. Accreditation Commission for Health Care
   b. Accreditation Council
   c. Alliance for Full Participation
   d. Accreditation

3. The _____ informally referred to as Obamacare, is a United States federal statute signed into law by President Barack Obama on March 23, 2010. The law (along with the Health Care and Education Reconciliation Act of 2010) is the principal health care reform legislation of the 111th United States Congress. PPACA requires individuals not covered by employer- or government-sponsored insurance plans to maintain minimal essential health insurance coverage or pay a penalty unless exempted for religious beliefs or financial hardship, a provision commonly referred to as the 'individual mandate'. The Act also reforms certain aspects of the private health insurance industry and public health insurance programs, increases insurance coverage of pre-existing conditions, expands access to insurance to 30 million Americans, and increases projected national medical spending while lowering projected Medicare spending.

   a. Prescription drug purchasing pool
   b. Protected health information
   c. Patient Protection and Affordable Care Act
   d. The Hospital Uninsured Patient Discount Act

4. . The _____ of 1985, is a law passed by the U.S. Congress and signed by President Reagan that, among other things, mandates an insurance program giving some employees the ability to continue health insurance coverage after leaving employment. _____ includes amendments to the Employee Retirement Income Security Act of 1974 (ERISA).

The law deals with a great variety of subjects, such as tobacco price supports, railroads, private pension plans, disability insurance, and the postal service , but it is perhaps best known for Title X, which amends the Internal Revenue Code and the Public Health Service Act to deny income tax deductions to employers for contributions to a group health plan unless such plan meets certain continuing coverage requirements.

a. 19NorDehydroepiandrosterone
b. Stockout
c. Supplier rating
d. Consolidated Omnibus Budget Reconciliation Act

5. The term quality management has a specific meaning within many business sectors. This specific definition, which does not aim to assure 'good quality' by the more general definition, but rather to ensure that an organization or product is consistent, can be considered to have four main components: quality planning, quality control, quality assurance and _____. Quality management is focused not only on product/service quality, but also the means to achieve it.

a. 19NorDehydroepiandrosterone
b. Quality improvement
c. Uncorrelated asymmetry
d. Uniform price auction

1. b
2. d
3. c
4. d
5. b

You can take the complete Online Interactive Chapter Practice Test

for 13. HIGH-QUALITY HEALTH CARE
on all key terms, persons, places, and concepts.

No Additional Costs

http://www.Cram101.com

Register, send an email request to Travis.Reese@Cram101.com to get your user Id and password.

Include your customer order number, and ISBN number from your studyguide Retailer.

14. MANAGING AND GOVERNING HEALTH CARE ORGANIZATIONS

Whitehall Study

Accountability

Governance

Corporification

Health

Nonprofit organization

Chief executive

Chief executive officer

Executive officer

Performance measurement

Medi-Cal

Medical home

Underinsurance

Management

Emotional intelligence

Service

Time management

Motivation

Program management

Environmental enrichment

Environmental protection

	Evidence-based management
	Case study

CHAPTER HIGHLIGHTS & NOTES: KEY TERMS, PEOPLE, PLACES, CONCEPTS

Whitehall Study	The original Whitehall Study investigated social determinants of health, specifically the cardiorespiratory disease prevalence and mortality rates among British male civil servants between the ages of 20 and 64. The initial prospective cohort study, the Whitehall I Study, examined over 18,000 male civil servants, and was conducted over a period of ten years, beginning in 1967. A second cohort study, the Whitehall II Study, examined the health of 10,308 civil servants aged 35 to 55, of whom two thirds were men and one third women. The response rate for Whitehall II was 73% in total, 74% for men and 71% for women. A long-term follow-up of study subjects from the first two phases is ongoing.
Accountability	Accountability is a concept in ethics and governance with several meanings. It is often used synonymously with such concepts as answerability, blameworthiness, liability, and other terms associated with the expectation of account-giving. As an aspect of governance, it has been central to discussions related to problems in the public sector, nonprofit and private (corporate) worlds.
Governance	Governance is the act of governing. It relates to decisions that define expectations, grant power, or verify performance. It consists of either a separate process or part of management or leadership processes.
Corporification	In pre-modern chemistry, corporification, was the practice of recovering spirits into the same body, or at least into a body nearly the same, as that which they had before their spiritualization.
Health	Health is the level of functional or metabolic efficiency of a living being. In humans, it is the general condition of a person's mind and body, usually meaning to be free from illness, injury or pain (as in 'good health' or 'healthy'). The World Health Organization (WHO) defined health in its broader sense in 1946 as 'a state of complete physical, mental, and social well-being and not merely the absence of disease or infirmity.' Although this definition has been subject to controversy, in particular as lacking operational value and because of the problem created by use of the word 'complete', it remains the most enduring .
Nonprofit organization	A nonprofit organization is an organization that does not distribute its surplus funds to owners or shareholders, but instead uses them to help pursue its goals.

14. MANAGING AND GOVERNING HEALTH CARE ORGANIZATIONS

	Examples of nonprofit organizations include charities (i.e., charitable organizations), trade unions, trade associations and public arts organizations. Most governments and government agencies meet this definition, but in most countries they are considered a separate type of organization and not counted as nonprofit organizations.
Chief executive	Chief Executive is a term used for certain gubernatorial offices, expressing the nature of their job being analogous to a head of government. Commonly used to refer to Presidential powers given by the constitution. As Chief Executive the president can: implement policy, supervise executive branch of government, prepare executive budget for submission to congress, and appoint and remove executive officials
	While in most cases there is another specific style, such as (lieutenant-)governor(-general), there are a few offices formally styled Chief Executive:•in the People's Republic of China, in two special administrative regions that were under foreign colonial rule until their recent transfer of sovereignty, where the chief executive are heads of the regions and heads of government:•in Mauritius, on Rodrigues island, since 12 October 2002 autonomy was granted:•New Zealand Antarctic Territory: while not a government, the Ross Dependency is a Crown entity managed by a Board of Directors and the Chair acts as the Chief Executive.
Chief executive officer	A Chief Executive Officer is the highest-ranking corporate officer (executive) or administrator in charge of total management of an organization. An individual appointed as a Chief executive officer of a corporation, company, organization, or agency typically reports to the board of directors. In British English, terms often used as synonyms for Chief executive officer are managing director (MD) and chief executive (CE).
Executive officer	An executive officer is generally a person responsible for running an organization, although the exact nature of the role varies depending on the organization. Administrative law
	While there is no clear line between executive or principal and inferior officers, principal officers are high-level officials in the executive branch of U.S. government such as department heads of independent agencies. In Humphrey's Executor v. United States, 295 U.S. 602 (1935), the Court distinguished between executive officers and quasi-legislative or quasi-judicial officers by stating that the former serve at the pleasure of the president and may be removed at his discretion.
Performance measurement	Performance measurement is a process for collecting and reporting information regarding the performance of an individual, group or organizations. It can involve looking at process/strategies in place, as well as whether outcomes are in line with what was intended or should have been achieved.
	Good performance is the criterion whereby an organization determines its capability to prevail.

Medi-Cal	The California Medical Assistance Program (Medi-Cal is the name of the California Medicaid welfare program serving low-income families, seniors, persons with disabilities, children in foster care, pregnant women, and certain low-income adults. It is jointly administered by the California Department of Health Care Services (DHCS) and the Centers for Medicare and Medicaid Services (CMS), with many services implemented at the local level mainly by the counties of California. Approximately 8.8 million citizens were enrolled in Medi-Cal for at least 1 month in 2009-10, or about 23% of California's population.
Medical home	The medical home, is a team based health care delivery model led by a physician that provides comprehensive and continuous medical care to patients with the goal of obtaining maximized health outcomes (American College of Physicians) (American Academy of Family Physicians). It is 'an approach to providing comprehensive primary care for children, youth and adults'. The provision of medical homes may allow better access to health care, increase satisfaction with care, and improve health.
Underinsurance	Condition of average (also called underinsurance in the U.S., or principal of average, subject to average, or pro rata condition of average in Commonwealth countries) is the insurance term used when calculating a payout against a claim where the policy undervalues the sum insured. In the event of partial loss, the amount paid against a claim will be in the same proportion as the value of the underinsurance. The formula used is where Payout is the amount paid out by the policy, Claim is the amount claimed against the policy after a loss, Sum Insured is the maximum amount to be paid out by the policy, and Current Value is the value the policy should be insured for.
Management	Management in all business and organizational activities is the act of getting people together to accomplish desired goals and objectives using available resources efficiently and effectively. Management comprises planning, organizing, staffing, leading or directing, and controlling an organization (a group of one or more people or entities) or effort for the purpose of accomplishing a goal. Resourcing encompasses the deployment and manipulation of human resources, financial resources, technological resources, and natural resources.
Emotional intelligence	Emotional intelligence describes the ability, capacity, skill or, in the case of the trait Emotional intelligence model, a self-perceived ability, to identify, assess, and manage the emotions of one's self, of others, and of groups. Different models have been proposed for the definition of Emotional intelligence and disagreement exists as to how the term should be used. Despite these disagreements, which are often highly technical, the ability Emotional intelligence and trait Emotional intelligence models (but not the mixed models) enjoy support in the literature and have successful applications in different domains.

14. MANAGING AND GOVERNING HEALTH CARE ORGANIZATIONS

Service	In economics, a service is an intangible commodity. More specifically, services are an intangible equivalent of economic goods.
	Service provision is often an economic activity where the buyer does not generally, except by exclusive contract, obtain exclusive ownership of the thing purchased.
Time management	Time management is the act or process of exercising conscious control over the amount of time spent on specific activities, especially to increase efficiency or productivity. Time management may be aided by a range of skills, tools, and techniques used to manage time when accomplishing specific tasks, projects and goals. This set encompasses a wide scope of activities, and these include planning, allocating, setting goals, delegation, analysis of time spent, monitoring, organizing, scheduling, and prioritizing.
Motivation	Motivation is the activation or energization of goal-oriented behavior. motivation may be intrinsic or extrinsic. The term is generally used for humans but, theoretically, it can also be used to describe the causes for animal behavior as well.
Program management	In the software industry, program management is an aspect of software product management.
	Program management is the process of managing several related projects, often with the intention of improving an organization's performance. In practice and in its aims it is often closely related to systems engineering and industrial engineering.
	The Program Manager has oversight of the purpose and status of all projects in a Program and can use this oversight to support project-level activity to ensure the overall program goals are likely to be met, possibly by providing a decision-making capacity that cannot be achieved at project level or by providing the Project Manager with a program perspective when required, or as a sounding board for ideas and approaches to solving project issues that have program impacts.
Environmental enrichment	Environmental enrichment concerns how the brain is affected by the stimulation of its information processing provided by its surroundings (including the opportunity to interact socially). Brains in richer, more stimulating environments, have increased numbers of synapses, and the dendrite arbors upon which they reside are more complex. This effect happens particularly during neurodevelopment, but also to a lesser degree in adulthood.
Environmental protection	Environmental protection is a practice of protecting the natural environment on individual, organizational or governmental levels, for the benefit of the natural environment and humans. Due to the pressures of population and technology, the biophysical environment is being degraded, sometimes permanently. This has been recognized, and governments have begun placing restraints on activities that cause environmental degradation.

Evidence-based management	Evidence-based management is an emerging movement to explicitly use the current, best evidence in management decision-making. Its roots are in evidence-based medicine, a quality movement to apply the scientific method to medical practice. Evidence-based management entails managerial decisions and organizational practices informed by the best available scientific evidence.
Case study	A case study is an intensive analysis of an individual unit (e.g., a person, group, or event) stressing developmental factors in relation to context. The case study is common in social sciences and life sciences. Case studies may be descriptive or explanatory.

1. _____ describes the ability, capacity, skill or, in the case of the trait _____ model, a self-perceived ability, to identify, assess, and manage the emotions of one's self, of others, and of groups. Different models have been proposed for the definition of _____ and disagreement exists as to how the term should be used. Despite these disagreements, which are often highly technical, the ability _____ and trait _____ models (but not the mixed models) enjoy support in the literature and have successful applications in different domains.

    a. Emotional intelligence
    b. Behavioral risk management
    c. Best current practice
    d. Best practice

2. An _____ is generally a person responsible for running an organization, although the exact nature of the role varies depending on the organization. Administrative law

    While there is no clear line between executive or principal and inferior officers, principal officers are high-level officials in the executive branch of U.S. government such as department heads of independent agencies. In Humphrey's Executor v. United States, 295 U.S. 602 (1935), the Court distinguished between _____s and quasi-legislative or quasi-judicial officers by stating that the former serve at the pleasure of the president and may be removed at his discretion.

    a. Independent director
    b. InfoSTEP
    c. Institute of Company Secretaries of India
    d. Executive officer

3. . _____ is the level of functional or metabolic efficiency of a living being.

14. MANAGING AND GOVERNING HEALTH CARE ORGANIZATIONS

In humans, it is the general condition of a person's mind and body, usually meaning to be free from illness, injury or pain (as in 'good _____' or 'healthy'). The World _____ Organization (WHO) defined _____ in its broader sense in 1946 as 'a state of complete physical, mental, and social well-being and not merely the absence of disease or infirmity.' Although this definition has been subject to controversy, in particular as lacking operational value and because of the problem created by use of the word 'complete', it remains the most enduring .

a. Sano Sansar Initiative
b. Sex differences in medicine
c. Sleep Cycle Alarm Clock
d. Health

4. The original _____ investigated social determinants of health, specifically the cardiorespiratory disease prevalence and mortality rates among British male civil servants between the ages of 20 and 64. The initial prospective cohort study, the Whitehall I Study, examined over 18,000 male civil servants, and was conducted over a period of ten years, beginning in 1967. A second cohort study, the Whitehall II Study, examined the health of 10,308 civil servants aged 35 to 55, of whom two thirds were men and one third women. The response rate for Whitehall II was 73% in total, 74% for men and 71% for women. A long-term follow-up of study subjects from the first two phases is ongoing.

a. 19NorDehydroepiandrosterone
b. Whitehall Study
c. 21-Hydroxylase
d. 3-MCPD

5. _____ is a concept in ethics and governance with several meanings. It is often used synonymously with such concepts as answerability, blameworthiness, liability, and other terms associated with the expectation of account-giving. As an aspect of governance, it has been central to discussions related to problems in the public sector, nonprofit and private (corporate) worlds.

a. Accountability in Research
b. Impeachment
c. Acanthamoeba
d. Accountability

ANSWER KEY
14. MANAGING AND GOVERNING HEALTH CARE ORGANIZATIONS

1. a
2. d
3. d
4. b
5. d

You can take the complete Online Interactive Chapter Practice Test

for 14. MANAGING AND GOVERNING HEALTH CARE ORGANIZATIONS
on all key terms, persons, places, and concepts.

No Additional Costs

http://www.Cram101.com

Register, send an email request to Travis.Reese@Cram101.com to get your user Id and password.

Include your customer order number, and ISBN number from your studyguide Retailer.

CHAPTER OUTLINE: KEY TERMS, PEOPLE, PLACES, CONCEPTS

	Initiative
	Health
	Human services
	National Committee for Quality Assurance
	Service
	Decision support
	Electronic health record
	Health record
	RECOrd
	HITECH Act
	Intermountain Healthcare
	Health information exchange
	Information exchange
	Health information technology
	Information technology
	Extended Care Health Option
	Kaiser Permanente
	Medicare
	Project
	Whitehall Study
	Gross domestic product

15. HEALTH INFORMATION TECHNOLOGY
CHAPTER OUTLINE: KEY TERMS, PEOPLE, PLACES, CONCEPTS

Standardization

Accountable care organization

Medi-Cal

Medical home

Patient-centered medical home

Institution

Population health

All-payer

Telehealth

Case study

CHAPTER HIGHLIGHTS & NOTES: KEY TERMS, PEOPLE, PLACES, CONCEPTS

Initiative	An initiative represents an enterprise's readiness to embark on a new venture. Generally speaking, the motivation for an initiative arises from a desire to accomplish something that would benefit the enterprise, such as improving productivity, reducing costs or increasing market share.
	A typical initiative is expressed as a process and includes metrics and time frames.
Health	Health is the level of functional or metabolic efficiency of a living being. In humans, it is the general condition of a person's mind and body, usually meaning to be free from illness, injury or pain (as in 'good health' or 'healthy'). The World Health Organization (WHO) defined health in its broader sense in 1946 as 'a state of complete physical, mental, and social well-being and not merely the absence of disease or infirmity.' Although this definition has been subject to controversy, in particular as lacking operational value and because of the problem created by use of the word 'complete', it remains the most enduring .

Human services	Human services refers to a variety of delivery systems such as social welfare services, education, mental health services, and other forms of healthcare. Human services professionals may provide services directly to clients or help clients access services. Human services professionals also manage agencies that provide these services.
National Committee for Quality Assurance	The National Committee for Quality Assurance is an independent 501(c)(3) non-profit organization in the United States designed to improve health care quality. It was established in 1990 with support from the Robert Wood Johnson Foundation. NCQA manages voluntary accreditation programs for individual physicians, health plans, and medical groups.
Service	In economics, a service is an intangible commodity. More specifically, services are an intangible equivalent of economic goods. Service provision is often an economic activity where the buyer does not generally, except by exclusive contract, obtain exclusive ownership of the thing purchased.
Decision support	A decision support system is a computer-based information system that supports business or organizational decision-making activities. DSSs serve the management, operations, and planning levels of an organization and help to make decisions, which may be rapidly changing and not easily specified in advance. Decision support systems can be either fully computerized, human or a combination of both.
Electronic health record	An electronic health record is an evolving concept defined as a systematic collection of electronic health information about individual patients or populations. It is a record in digital format that is theoretically capable of being shared across different health care settings. In some cases this sharing can occur by way of network-connected enterprise-wide information systems and other information networks or exchanges.
Health record	The terms medical record, health record, and medical chart are used somewhat interchangeably to describe the systematic documentation of a single patient's medical history and care across time within one particular health care provider's jurisdiction. The medical record includes a variety of types of 'notes' entered over time by health care professionals, recording observations and administration of drugs and therapies, orders for the administration of drugs and therapies, test results, x-rays, reports, etc. The maintenance of complete and accurate medical records is a requirement of health care providers and is generally enforced as a licensing or certification prerequisite.
RECOrd	RECOrd is a Local Biological Records Centre (LRC) serving Cheshire, Halton, Warrington and Wirral (including the vice-county 'pan-handle' boundary around Stockport) - 'The Cheshire region'. It provides a local facility for the storage, validation and usage of Cheshire-based biological data under the National Biodiversity Network (NBN) project.

15. HEALTH INFORMATION TECHNOLOGY

	It is one of a number of local Biological Records Centres across Britain which together aim to give complete geographic coverage of the UK. The organisation is housed in Oakfield House at Chester Zoo.
HITECH Act	The Health Information Technology for Economic and Clinical Health Act, abbreviated HITECH Act, was enacted under Title XIII of the American Recovery and Reinvestment Act of 2009 . Under the HITECH Act, the United States Department of Health and Human Services is spending $25.9 billion to promote and expand the adoption of health information technology. The Washington Post reported the inclusion of 'as much as $36.5 billion in spending to create a nationwide network of electronic health records.' At the time it was enacted, it was considered 'the most important piece of health care legislation to be passed in the last 20 to 30 years' and the 'foundation for health care reform.' The National Coordinator for Health Information Technology, Dr. Farzad Mostashari, has explained: 'You need information to be able to do population health management.
Intermountain Healthcare	Intermountain Health Care, Inc., officially doing business as as Intermountain Healthcare, is a non-profit healthcare system and is the largest healthcare provider in the Intermountain West. Until 2005 it known as Intermountain Health Care or more commonly IHC; it is now. Intermountain Healthcare is headquartered in Salt Lake City, Utah, and currently employs over 32,000 people.
Health information exchange	Health information exchange is the mobilization of healthcare information electronically across organizations within a region, community or hospital system. Health information exchange provides the capability to electronically move clinical information among disparate health care information systems while maintaining the meaning of the information being exchanged. The goal of Health information exchange is to facilitate access to and retrieval of clinical data to provide safer and more timely, efficient, effective, and equitable patient-centered care.
Information exchange	Information exchange is an informal term that can either refer to bidirectional information transmission/information transfer in telecommunications and computer science or communication seen from a system-theoretic or information-theoretic point of view. Information exchange is also used to describe the process of learning and the efficiency of the learning.
Health information technology	Health information technology provides the umbrella framework to describe the comprehensive management of health information across computerized systems and its secure exchange between consumers, providers, government and quality entities, and insurers. Health information technology is in general increasingly viewed as the most promising tool for improving the overall quality, safety and efficiency of the health delivery system (Chaudhry et al., 2006).

	Broad and consistent utilization of Health information technology will:•Improve health care quality;•Prevent medical errors;•Reduce health care costs;•Increase administrative efficiencies;•Decrease paperwork; and•Expand access to affordable care
	Interoperable Health information technology will improve individual patient care, but it will also bring many public health benefits including:•Early detection of infectious disease outbreaks around the country;•Improved tracking of chronic disease management; and•Evaluation of health care based on value enabled by the collection of de-identified price and quality information that can be compared Concepts and Definitions
	Health information technology is 'the application of information processing involving both computer hardware and software that deals with the storage, retrieval, sharing, and use of health care information, data, and knowledge for communication and decision making' (Brailer, & Thompson, 2004).
Information technology	Information Technology is the branch of engineering that deals with the use of computers and telecommunications to store, retrieve and transmit information.
Extended Care Health Option	The Extended Care Health Option is a supplemental coverage program offered by TRICARE to dependents of members of the Uniformed services of the United States with a qualifying disability. Eligibility
	Extended Care Health Option benefits are available with a qualifying condition to a TRICARE-eligible child or spouse of an active duty uniformed service member.
	The following are qualifying conditions under Extended Care Health Option:•Moderate or severe mental retardation•A serious physical disability•An extraordinary physical or psychological condition of such complexity that the beneficiary is homebound Extended Care Health Option Enrollment/Registration
	TRICARE Extended Care Health Option requires all eligible beneficiaries do the following:•Present evidence that the sponsor is an active duty service member in one of the Uniform Services•Enroll in the Exceptional Family Member Program (EFMP) that is available through their service branch•Submit the required Enrollment Forms: DD Form 2792 Exceptional Family Member Medical Summary, DD Form 2792-1 Exceptional Family Member Special Education/Early Intervention•Register with their regional contractor to obtain Extended Care Health Option benefit authorization
	For more information about the EFMP, Department of Defense beneficiaries may visit the Military Homefront Website.

15. HEALTH INFORMATION TECHNOLOGY

Kaiser Permanente	Kaiser Permanente is an integrated managed care consortium, based in Oakland, California, United States, founded in 1945 by industrialist Henry J. Kaiser and physician Sidney Garfield. Kaiser Permanente is made up of three distinct groups of entities: the Kaiser Foundation Health Plan and its regional operating subsidiaries; Kaiser Foundation Hospitals; and the autonomous regional Permanente Medical Groups. As of 2006, Kaiser Permanente operates in nine states and the District of Columbia, and is the largest managed care organization in the United States.
Medicare	Medicare is the unofficial name for Canada's publicly funded universal health insurance system. The formal terminology for the insurance system is provided by the Canada Health Act and the health insurance legislation of the individual provinces and territories. Under the terms of the Canada Health Act, all 'insured persons' (basically, legal residents of Canada, including permanent residents) are entitled to receive 'insured services' without copayment.
Project	A project in business and science is typically defined as a collaborative enterprise, frequently involving research or design, that is carefully planned to achieve a particular aim. Projects can be further defined as temporary rather than permanent social systems that are constituted by teams within or across organizations to accomplish particular tasks under time constraints. Overview The word project comes from the Latin word projectum from the Latin verb proicere, 'before an action' which in turn comes from pro-, which denotes precedence, something that comes before something else in time and iacere, 'to do'.
Whitehall Study	The original Whitehall Study investigated social determinants of health, specifically the cardiorespiratory disease prevalence and mortality rates among British male civil servants between the ages of 20 and 64. The initial prospective cohort study, the Whitehall I Study, examined over 18,000 male civil servants, and was conducted over a period of ten years, beginning in 1967. A second cohort study, the Whitehall II Study, examined the health of 10,308 civil servants aged 35 to 55, of whom two thirds were men and one third women. The response rate for Whitehall II was 73% in total, 74% for men and 71% for women. A long-term follow-up of study subjects from the first two phases is ongoing.
Gross domestic product	Gross domestic product is the market value of all officially recognized final goods and services produced within a country in a year, or other given period of time. gross domestic product per capita is often considered an indicator of a country's standard of living. gross domestic product per capita is not a measure of personal income .
Standardization	Standardization is to implement guidelines, a design, or measurements in order to obtain solutions to an otherwise disorganized system.

	The goals of standardization can be to help with independence of single suppliers (commoditization), compatibility, interoperability, safety, repeatability, or quality. In social sciences, including economics, the idea of standardization is close to the solution for a coordination problem, a situation in which all parties can realize mutual gains, but only by making mutually consistent decisions.
Accountable care organization	An accountable care organization is a healthcare organization characterized by a payment and care delivery model that seeks to tie provider reimbursements to quality metrics and reductions in the total cost of care for an assigned population of patients. A group of coordinated health care providers forms an Accountable care organization, which then provides care to a group of patients. The Accountable care organization may use a range of payment models (capitation, fee-for-service with asymmetric or symmetric shared savings, etc)..
Medi-Cal	The California Medical Assistance Program (Medi-Cal is the name of the California Medicaid welfare program serving low-income families, seniors, persons with disabilities, children in foster care, pregnant women, and certain low-income adults. It is jointly administered by the California Department of Health Care Services (DHCS) and the Centers for Medicare and Medicaid Services (CMS), with many services implemented at the local level mainly by the counties of California. Approximately 8.8 million citizens were enrolled in Medi-Cal for at least 1 month in 2009-10, or about 23% of California's population.
Medical home	The medical home, is a team based health care delivery model led by a physician that provides comprehensive and continuous medical care to patients with the goal of obtaining maximized health outcomes (American College of Physicians) (American Academy of Family Physicians). It is 'an approach to providing comprehensive primary care for children, youth and adults'. The provision of medical homes may allow better access to health care, increase satisfaction with care, and improve health.
Patient-centered medical home	The medical home, also known as the patient-centered medical home is a team based health care delivery model led by a physician, P.A., or N.P. that provides comprehensive and continuous medical care to patients with the goal of obtaining maximized health outcomes (American College of Physicians) (American Academy of Family Physicians). It is 'an approach to providing comprehensive primary care for children, youth and adults'. The provision of medical homes may allow better access to health care, increase satisfaction with care, and improve health.
Institution	An institution is any structure or mechanism of social order and cooperation governing the behavior of a set of individuals within a given human community. Institutions are identified with a social purpose and permanence, transcending individual human lives and intention by enforcing rules that governs cooperative human behavior.

15. HEALTH INFORMATION TECHNOLOGY

Population health	Population health has been defined as 'the health outcomes of a group of individuals, including the distribution of such outcomes within the group.' It is an approach to health that aims to improve the health of an entire population. One major step in achieving this aim is to reduce health inequities among population groups. Population health seeks to step beyond the individual-level focus of mainstream medicine and public health by addressing a broad range of factors that impact health on a population-level, such as environment, social structure, resource distribution, etc.
All-payer	All-payer rate setting is a rate-setting system under which all third parties pay the same price for services at a given hospital. The system does not imply that charges are the same for every hospital. It can be used to increase the market power of payers (such as private and/or public insurance companies) to mitigate inflation in health care costs.
Telehealth	Telehealth is the delivery of health-related services and information via telecommunications technologies. Telehealth could be as simple as two health professionals discussing a case over the telephone or as sophisticated as doing robotic surgery between facilities at different ends of the globe. Telehealth is an expansion of telemedicine, and unlike telemedicine (which more narrowly focuses on the curative aspect) it encompasses preventative, promotive and curative aspects.
Case study	A case study is an intensive analysis of an individual unit (e.g., a person, group, or event) stressing developmental factors in relation to context. The case study is common in social sciences and life sciences. Case studies may be descriptive or explanatory.

1. In economics, a _____ is an intangible commodity. More specifically, _____s are an intangible equivalent of economic goods.

   _____ provision is often an economic activity where the buyer does not generally, except by exclusive contract, obtain exclusive ownership of the thing purchased.

   a. Service
   b. Stockout
   c. Supplier rating
   d. Supply chain

2. . An _____ represents an enterprise's readiness to embark on a new venture.

Generally speaking, the motivation for an _____ arises from a desire to accomplish something that would benefit the enterprise, such as improving productivity, reducing costs or increasing market share.

A typical _____ is expressed as a process and includes metrics and time frames.

a. International Project Management Association
b. Initiative
c. Alexander Laufer
d. Organizational project management

3. _____ is the unofficial name for Canada's publicly funded universal health insurance system. The formal terminology for the insurance system is provided by the Canada Health Act and the health insurance legislation of the individual provinces and territories.

Under the terms of the Canada Health Act, all 'insured persons' (basically, legal residents of Canada, including permanent residents) are entitled to receive 'insured services' without copayment.

a. PAMI
b. Public health system in India
c. Medicare
d. Socialized medicine

4. The _____ is an independent 501(c)(3) non-profit organization in the United States designed to improve health care quality. It was established in 1990 with support from the Robert Wood Johnson Foundation. NCQA manages voluntary accreditation programs for individual physicians, health plans, and medical groups.

a. Pakistan Medical and Dental Council
b. National Committee for Quality Assurance
c. Scope of practice
d. Smoking ban

5. _____ is the level of functional or metabolic efficiency of a living being. In humans, it is the general condition of a person's mind and body, usually meaning to be free from illness, injury or pain (as in 'good _____' or 'healthy'). The World _____ Organization (WHO) defined _____ in its broader sense in 1946 as 'a state of complete physical, mental, and social well-being and not merely the absence of disease or infirmity.' Although this definition has been subject to controversy, in particular as lacking operational value and because of the problem created by use of the word 'complete', it remains the most enduring .

a. Sano Sansar Initiative
b. Health
c. Sleep Cycle Alarm Clock
d. mortality ratio

1. a
2. b
3. c
4. b
5. b

You can take the complete Online Interactive Chapter Practice Test

for 15. HEALTH INFORMATION TECHNOLOGY
on all key terms, persons, places, and concepts.

No Additional Costs

http://www.Cram101.com

Register, send an email request to Travis.Reese@Cram101.com to get your user Id and password.

Include your customer order number, and ISBN number from your studyguide Retailer.

16. THE FUTURE OF HEALTH CARE DELIVERY AND HEALTH POLICY

CHAPTER OUTLINE: KEY TERMS, PEOPLE, PLACES, CONCEPTS

_____ | Delphi method

_____ | Hypothetico-deductive model

_____ | Robotics

_____ | Health

_____ | Health care

_____ | Telehealth

_____ | Whitehall Study

_____ | Consumer

_____ | Case study

_____ | Individual mandate

_____ | Fertility clinic

_____ | Health insurance

_____ | Health insurance exchange

_____ | Catastrophic

_____ | Diacritic

_____ | Medicare

_____ | High-risk pool

_____ | Medicaid

_____ | Health system

_____ | Performance improvement

_____ | Long-term care

Accreditation

Association

Health Officers

Behavioral health

Bundled payment

Combat Support Hospital

Charity care

Chronic

Chronic care

Alternative medicine

Copayment

Quality improvement

Service

Employee Retirement Income Security Act

Human services

Income

Medi-Cal

Disproportionate share hospital

Electronic health record

Emotional intelligence

Health record

RECOrd

Environmental enrichment

Environmental protection

End-of-life care

Evidence-based management

Fee-for-service

Food

Management

Group Health

Governance

Accountability

Health Insurance Portability and Accountability Act

Hospice

Hospice care

Indemnity

Horizontal integration

Information technology

Integrated delivery system

Vertical integration

Cranial root of accessory nerve

Managed care

	Public health
	Quality assurance
	Nurse Practitioner
	Intermountain Healthcare
	Institution
	Medical home
	Palliative
	Palliative care
	Patient-centered medical home
	Preferred provider organization
	Primary care
	Public hospital
	Resource-based relative value scale
	Risk
	Waterlow score
	Joint Commission
	Socialized medicine
	Tertiary
	Tertiary care
	Coalition
	Initiative

16. THE FUTURE OF HEALTH CARE DELIVERY AND HEALTH POLICY

Delphi method	The Delphi method is a structured communication technique, originally developed as a systematic, interactive forecasting method which relies on a panel of experts.
	In the standard version, the experts answer questionnaires in two or more rounds. After each round, a facilitator provides an anonymous summary of the experts' forecasts from the previous round as well as the reasons they provided for their judgments.
Hypothetico-deductive model	The hypothetico-deductive model, first so-named by William Whewell, is a proposed description of scientific method. According to it, scientific inquiry proceeds by formulating a hypothesis in a form that could conceivably be falsified by a test on observable data. A test that could and does run contrary to predictions of the hypothesis is taken as a falsification of the hypothesis.
Robotics	There are many conventions used in the Robotics research field
	Lines are very important in Robotics because:
	· They model joint axes: a revolute joint makes any connected rigid body rotate about the line of its axis; a prismatic joint makes the connected rigid body translate along its axis line.
Health	Health is the level of functional or metabolic efficiency of a living being. In humans, it is the general condition of a person's mind and body, usually meaning to be free from illness, injury or pain (as in 'good health' or 'healthy'). The World Health Organization (WHO) defined health in its broader sense in 1946 as 'a state of complete physical, mental, and social well-being and not merely the absence of disease or infirmity.' Although this definition has been subject to controversy, in particular as lacking operational value and because of the problem created by use of the word 'complete', it remains the most enduring .
Health care	Health care is the diagnosis, treatment, and prevention of disease, illness, injury, and other physical and mental impairments in humans. Health care is delivered by practitioners in medicine, chiropractic, dentistry, nursing, pharmacy, allied health, and other care providers. It refers to the work done in providing primary care, secondary care and tertiary care, as well as in public health.
Telehealth	Telehealth is the delivery of health-related services and information via telecommunications technologies. Telehealth could be as simple as two health professionals discussing a case over the telephone or as sophisticated as doing robotic surgery between facilities at different ends of the globe.
	Telehealth is an expansion of telemedicine, and unlike telemedicine (which more narrowly focuses on the curative aspect) it encompasses preventative, promotive and curative aspects.

Whitehall Study	The original Whitehall Study investigated social determinants of health, specifically the cardiorespiratory disease prevalence and mortality rates among British male civil servants between the ages of 20 and 64. The initial prospective cohort study, the Whitehall I Study, examined over 18,000 male civil servants, and was conducted over a period of ten years, beginning in 1967. A second cohort study, the Whitehall II Study, examined the health of 10,308 civil servants aged 35 to 55, of whom two thirds were men and one third women. The response rate for Whitehall II was 73% in total, 74% for men and 71% for women. A long-term follow-up of study subjects from the first two phases is ongoing.
Consumer	Consumers are organisms of an ecological food chain that receive their energy by consuming other organisms. These organisms are formally referred to as heterotrophs, which includes animals, bacteria and fungus. Such organisms may consume by various means, including predation, parasitization, and biodegradation.
Case study	A case study is an intensive analysis of an individual unit (e.g., a person, group, or event) stressing developmental factors in relation to context. The case study is common in social sciences and life sciences. Case studies may be descriptive or explanatory.
Individual mandate	An individual mandate is a requirement by a government that certain individual citizens purchase a good or service. In the United States, an early federal mandate in the Militia Acts of 1792 required every 'free able-bodied white male citizen' between the ages of 18 and 45, with a few occupational exceptions, to purchase a weapon and ammunition. A modern individual mandate, known as a health insurance mandate, sets up a requirement that an individual either buy health insurance or face a penalty.
Fertility clinic	Fertility clinics are staffed medical clinics that assist couples, and , who want to become parents but for medical reasons have been unable to achieve this goal via the natural course. Clinics apply a number of tests and sometimes very advanced medical procedures to obtain the desired conceptions and pregnancies. For the male, semen collection is a standard diagnostic test to ascertain problems with the semen quality.
Health insurance	Health insurance is insurance against the risk of incurring medical expenses among individuals. By estimating the overall risk of health care and health system expenses among a targeted group, an insurer can develop a routine finance structure, such as a monthly premium or payroll tax, to ensure that money is available to pay for the health care benefits specified in the insurance agreement. The benefit is administered by a central organization such as a government agency, private business, or not-for-profit entity.

16. THE FUTURE OF HEALTH CARE DELIVERY AND HEALTH POLICY

Health insurance exchange	A health insurance exchange is a set of government-regulated and standardized health care plans in the United States, from which individuals may purchase health insurance eligible for federal subsidies. All exchanges must be fully certified and operational by January 1, 2014, under federal law. Acronym HIX (Health Insurance Exchange) is emerging as the de facto acronym across state and federal government stakeholders, and the private sector technology and service providers that are helping states build their exchanges.
Catastrophic	A catastrophe is an extremely large-scale disaster, a horrible event. It may also refer to: · Catastrophe bond, a risk-linked security used to share risks with bond investors · Catastrophe (book), a non-fiction book by Dick Morris and Eileen McGann · Catastrophe (drama), the climax and resolution of a plot in ancient Greek drama and poems · Catastrophe modeling, in Insurance, projecting of the cost of losses due to a catastrophic event · Catastrophe , a 1982 short play by Samuel Beckett · Catastrophe theory, a field of mathematics that studies how the behavior of dynamic systems can change drastically with small variations · Microtubular catastrophe, a feature of the cytoskeleton in eukaryotic cells · Catastrophe (TV series), a five-part science series on Channel 4 a bridge collapses) · catastrophic, a difficulty rating in Dance Dance Revolution · catastrophic, a metal band and side project of Obituary's guitarist Trevor Peres '
Diacritic	A diacritic is an ancillary glyph added to a letter, 'distinguishing'). diacritic is both an adjective and a noun, whereas diacritical is only an adjective.
Medicare	Medicare is the unofficial name for Canada's publicly funded universal health insurance system. The formal terminology for the insurance system is provided by the Canada Health Act and the health insurance legislation of the individual provinces and territories. Under the terms of the Canada Health Act, all 'insured persons' (basically, legal residents of Canada, including permanent residents) are entitled to receive 'insured services' without copayment.
High-risk pool	A high-risk pool is a health insurance provider, often operated by a government entity, for people on the individual health insurance market who are deemed too risky by private insurers.
Medicaid	Medicaid is the United States health program for families and individuals with low income and resources. It is a means-tested program that is jointly funded by the state and federal governments, and is managed by the states. People served by Medicaid are U.S.

Health system	A health system, also sometimes referred to as health care system or healthcare system is the organization of people, institutions, and resources to deliver health care services to meet the health needs of target populations.
	There is a wide variety of health systems around the world, with as many histories and organizational structures as there are nations. In some countries, health system planning is distributed among market participants.
Performance improvement	Performance improvement is the concept of measuring the output of a particular process or procedure, then modifying the process or procedure in order to increase the output, increase efficiency, or increase the effectiveness of the process or procedure.
Long-term care	Long-term care is a variety of services which help meet both the medical and non-medical needs of people with a chronic illness or disability who cannot care for themselves for long periods of time.
	It is common for long-term care to provide custodial and non-skilled care, such as assisting with normal daily tasks like dressing, bathing, and using the bathroom. Increasingly, long-term care involves providing a level of medical care that requires the expertise of skilled practitioners to address the often multiple chronic conditions associated with older populations.
Accreditation	Accreditation is a process in which certification of competency, authority, or credibility is presented.
	Organizations that issue credentials or certify third parties against official standards are themselves formally accredited by accreditation bodies (such as UKAS); hence they are sometimes known as 'accredited certification bodies'. The accreditation process ensures that their certification practices are acceptable, typically meaning that they are competent to test and certify third parties, behave ethically and employ suitable quality assurance.
Association	In statistics, an association is any relationship between two measured quantities that renders them statistically dependent. The term 'association' refers broadly to any such relationship, whereas the narrower term 'correlation' refers to a linear relationship between two quantities.
	There are many statistical measures of association that can be used to infer the presence or absence of an association in a sample of data.
Health Officers	Health Officers
	Health Officers is a common term used in the United States and elsewhere for public health officials. Public health officials may serve at the global, federal, state, county, or municipal level. Health officers are concerned with protecting and improving the health of communities, states, nations and populations.

16. THE FUTURE OF HEALTH CARE DELIVERY AND HEALTH POLICY

Behavioral health	Behavioral health is a general term now commonly used in place of the older term mental health. Like similar terms such as mental health and physical health, behavioral health is a basic English term which derives its meaning from the simple association between noun and adjective. Normal variations in the definition of such terms may be expected, given common variations seen in the component words 'behavioral' and 'health'.
Bundled payment	Bundled payment, also known as episode-based payment, episode payment, episode-of-care payment, case rate, evidence-based case rate, global bundled payment, global payment, package pricing, or packaged pricing, is defined as the reimbursement of health care providers (such as hospitals and physicians) 'on the basis of expected costs for clinically-defined episodes of care.' It has been described as 'a middle ground' between fee-for-service reimbursement (in which providers are paid for each service rendered to a patient) and capitation (in which providers are paid a 'lump sum' per patient regardless of how many services the patient receives). Bundled payments have been proposed in the health care reform debate in the United States as a strategy for reducing health care costs, especially during the Obama administration (2009-present). In the mid-1980s, it was believed that Medicare's then-new hospital prospective payment system using diagnosis-related groups may have led to hospitals' discharging patients to post-hospital care (e.g., skilled nursing facilities) more quickly than appropriate in order to save money.
Combat Support Hospital	A Combat Support Hospital is a type of field hospital. The Combat Support Hospital is a United States military mobile hospital delivered to the Corps Support Area in standard military-owned Demountable Containers (MILVAN) cargo containers and assembled by the staff into a tent hospital to treat wounded soldiers. The size of the hospital is almost infinitely expandable by chaining tents together, but it will typically deploy with between 16 and 256 operational hospital beds.
Charity care	In the United States, charity care is health care provided for free or at reduced prices to low income patients. The percentage of doctors providing charity care dropped from 76% in 1996-97 to 68% in 2004-2005. Potential reasons for the decline include changes in physician practice patterns and increasing financial pressures. In 2006, Senate investigators found that many hospitals did not inform patients that charity care was available.
Chronic	A chronic condition is a human health condition or disease that is persistent or otherwise long-lasting in its effects. The term chronic is usually applied when the course of the disease lasts for more than three months. Common chronic diseases include arthritis, asthma, cancer, COPD, diabetes and HIV/AIDS. In medicine, the opposite of chronic is acute.

Chronic care	Chronic care refers to medical care which addresses preexisting or long term illness, as opposed to acute care which is concerned with short term or severe illness of brief duration. Chronic medical conditions include, but are not limited to, asthma, emphysema, chronic bronchitis, congestive heart disease, cirrhosis of the liver, hypertension and depression. Chronic medical care accounts for more than 75% of health care dollars spent in the US. Nursing care for the chronically ill A nurse has to be qualified to handle all the needs of a chronic client.
Alternative medicine	Alternative medicine is any practice claiming to heal 'that does not fall within the realm of conventional medicine.' It may be based on historical or cultural traditions, rather than on scientific evidence. Alternative medicine is frequently grouped with complementary medicine or integrative medicine, which, in general, refers to the same interventions when used in conjunction with mainstream techniques, under the umbrella term complementary and alternative medicine, or CAM. Critics maintain that the terms 'complementary' and 'alternative medicine' are deceptive euphemisms meant to give an impression of medical authority. A 1998 systematic review of studies assessing its prevalence in 13 countries concluded that about 31% of cancer patients use some form of complementary and alternative medicine.
Copayment	In the United States, copayment is accessed. It is technically a form of coinsurance, but is defined differently in health insurance where a coinsurance is a percentage payment after the deductible up to a certain limit. It must be paid before any policy benefit is payable by an insurance company.
Quality improvement	The term quality management has a specific meaning within many business sectors. This specific definition, which does not aim to assure 'good quality' by the more general definition, but rather to ensure that an organization or product is consistent, can be considered to have four main components: quality planning, quality control, quality assurance and quality improvement. Quality management is focused not only on product/service quality, but also the means to achieve it.
Service	In economics, a service is an intangible commodity. More specifically, services are an intangible equivalent of economic goods. Service provision is often an economic activity where the buyer does not generally, except by exclusive contract, obtain exclusive ownership of the thing purchased.
Employee Retirement Income Security Act	The Employee Retirement Income Security Act of 1974 is a federal law which establishes minimum standards for pension plans in private industry and provides for extensive rules on the federal income tax effects of transactions associated with employee benefit plans.

16. THE FUTURE OF HEALTH CARE DELIVERY AND HEALTH POLICY

	Employee Retirement Income Security Act was enacted to protect the interests of employee benefit plan participants and their beneficiaries by:•Requiring the disclosure of financial and other information concerning the plan to beneficiaries;•Establishing standards of conduct for plan fiduciaries;•Providing for appropriate remedies and access to the federal courts
	Employee Retirement Income Security Act is sometimes used to refer to the full body of laws regulating employee benefit plans, which are found mainly in the Internal Revenue Code and Employee Retirement Income Security Act itself.
	Responsibility for the interpretation and enforcement of Employee Retirement Income Security Act is divided among the Department of Labor, the Department of the Treasury (particularly the Internal Revenue Service), and the Pension Benefit Guaranty Corporation.
Human services	Human services refers to a variety of delivery systems such as social welfare services, education, mental health services, and other forms of healthcare. Human services professionals may provide services directly to clients or help clients access services. Human services professionals also manage agencies that provide these services.
Income	Income is the consumption and savings opportunity gained by an entity within a specified timeframe, which is generally expressed in monetary terms. However, for households and individuals, 'income is the sum of all the wages, salaries, profits, interests payments, rents and other forms of earnings received... in a given period of time.'
	In the field of public economics, the term may refer to the accumulation of both monetary and non-monetary consumption ability, with the former (monetary) being used as a proxy for total income. Increase in income
	Income per capita has been increasing steadily in almost every country.
Medi-Cal	The California Medical Assistance Program (Medi-Cal is the name of the California Medicaid welfare program serving low-income families, seniors, persons with disabilities, children in foster care, pregnant women, and certain low-income adults. It is jointly administered by the California Department of Health Care Services (DHCS) and the Centers for Medicare and Medicaid Services (CMS), with many services implemented at the local level mainly by the counties of California. Approximately 8.8 million citizens were enrolled in Medi-Cal for at least 1 month in 2009-10, or about 23% of California's population.
Disproportionate share hospital	The United States government provides funding to hospitals that treat indigent patients through the Disproportionate Share Hospital programs, under which facilities are able to receive at least partial compensation.

	Although 3,109 hospitals receive this adjustment, Medicare Disproportionate share hospital payments are highly concentrated. Ninety three percent of total Disproportionate share hospital payments go to large hospitals in urban areas and teaching hospitals receive about 65 percent of all Disproportionate share hospital payments.
Electronic health record	An electronic health record is an evolving concept defined as a systematic collection of electronic health information about individual patients or populations. It is a record in digital format that is theoretically capable of being shared across different health care settings. In some cases this sharing can occur by way of network-connected enterprise-wide information systems and other information networks or exchanges.
Emotional intelligence	Emotional intelligence describes the ability, capacity, skill or, in the case of the trait Emotional intelligence model, a self-perceived ability, to identify, assess, and manage the emotions of one's self, of others, and of groups. Different models have been proposed for the definition of Emotional intelligence and disagreement exists as to how the term should be used. Despite these disagreements, which are often highly technical, the ability Emotional intelligence and trait Emotional intelligence models (but not the mixed models) enjoy support in the literature and have successful applications in different domains.
Health record	The terms medical record, health record, and medical chart are used somewhat interchangeably to describe the systematic documentation of a single patient's medical history and care across time within one particular health care provider's jurisdiction. The medical record includes a variety of types of 'notes' entered over time by health care professionals, recording observations and administration of drugs and therapies, orders for the administration of drugs and therapies, test results, x-rays, reports, etc. The maintenance of complete and accurate medical records is a requirement of health care providers and is generally enforced as a licensing or certification prerequisite.
RECOrd	RECOrd is a Local Biological Records Centre (LRC) serving Cheshire, Halton, Warrington and Wirral (including the vice-county 'pan-handle' boundary around Stockport) - 'The Cheshire region'. It provides a local facility for the storage, validation and usage of Cheshire-based biological data under the National Biodiversity Network (NBN) project. It is one of a number of local Biological Records Centres across Britain which together aim to give complete geographic coverage of the UK. The organisation is housed in Oakfield House at Chester Zoo.
Environmental enrichment	Environmental enrichment concerns how the brain is affected by the stimulation of its information processing provided by its surroundings (including the opportunity to interact socially). Brains in richer, more stimulating environments, have increased numbers of synapses, and the dendrite arbors upon which they reside are more complex.

16. THE FUTURE OF HEALTH CARE DELIVERY AND HEALTH POLICY

Environmental protection	Environmental protection is a practice of protecting the natural environment on individual, organizational or governmental levels, for the benefit of the natural environment and humans. Due to the pressures of population and technology, the biophysical environment is being degraded, sometimes permanently. This has been recognized, and governments have begun placing restraints on activities that cause environmental degradation.
End-of-life care	In medicine, end-of-life care refers to medical care not only of patients in the final hours or days of their lives, but more broadly, medical care of all those with a terminal illness or terminal condition that has become advanced, progressive and incurable. Regarding cancer care the United States National Cancer Institute writes: When a patient's health care team determines that the cancer can no longer be controlled, medical testing and cancer treatment often stop. But the patient's care continues.
Evidence-based management	Evidence-based management is an emerging movement to explicitly use the current, best evidence in management decision-making. Its roots are in evidence-based medicine, a quality movement to apply the scientific method to medical practice. Evidence-based management entails managerial decisions and organizational practices informed by the best available scientific evidence.
Fee-for-service	Fee-for-service is a payment model where services are unbundled and paid for separately. In health care, it gives an incentive for physicians to provide more treatments because payment is dependent on the quantity of care, rather than quality of care. Similarly, when patients are shielded from paying (cost-sharing) by health insurance coverage, they are incentivized to welcome any medical service that might do some good.
Food	Food is any substance consumed to provide nutritional support for the body. It is usually of plant or animal origin, and contains essential nutrients, such as carbohydrates, fats, proteins, vitamins, or minerals. The substance is ingested by an organism and assimilated by the organism's cells in an effort to produce energy, maintain life, or stimulate growth.
Management	Management in all business and organizational activities is the act of getting people together to accomplish desired goals and objectives using available resources efficiently and effectively. Management comprises planning, organizing, staffing, leading or directing, and controlling an organization (a group of one or more people or entities) or effort for the purpose of accomplishing a goal. Resourcing encompasses the deployment and manipulation of human resources, financial resources, technological resources, and natural resources.
Group Health	Group Health Cooperative, more commonly known as Group Health, is a Seattle, Washington based nonprofit healthcare organization.

	Established in 1945, it today provides coverage and care for about 700,000 people in Washington and Idaho and is one of the largest private employers in Washington. Patients who receive care at its medical centers are provided Web access to their medical records, secure emailing with doctors and nurses and the ability to fill prescriptions online that are mailed to homes without a shipping charge.
Governance	Governance is the act of governing. It relates to decisions that define expectations, grant power, or verify performance. It consists of either a separate process or part of management or leadership processes.
Accountability	Accountability is a concept in ethics and governance with several meanings. It is often used synonymously with such concepts as answerability, blameworthiness, liability, and other terms associated with the expectation of account-giving. As an aspect of governance, it has been central to discussions related to problems in the public sector, nonprofit and private (corporate) worlds.
Health Insurance Portability and Accountability Act	The Administrative Simplification provisions of the Health Insurance Portability and Accountability Act of 1996 (HIPAA, Title II) require the Department of Health and Human Services (HHS) to adopt national standards for electronic health care transactions and national identifiers for providers, health plans, and employers. To date, the implementation of HIPAA standards has increased the use of electronic data interchange. Provisions under the Affordable Care Act of 2010 will further these increases and include requirements to adopt: operating rules for each of the HIPAA covered transactionsa unique, standard Health Plan Identifier (HPID)a standard and operating rules for electronic funds transfer (EFT) and electronic remittance advice (RA) and claims attachments.In addition, health plans will be required to certify their compliance. The Act provides for substantial penalties for failures to certify or comply with the new standards and operating rules.
Hospice	Hospice is a type of care and a philosophy of care that focuses on the palliation of a terminally ill patient's symptoms. These symptoms can be physical, emotional, spiritual or social in nature. Hospice care focuses on bringing comfort, self-respect, and tranquility to the dying patient.
Hospice care	Hospice care is a type and philosophy of care that focuses on the palliative care of a terminally ill or seriously ill patient's pain and symptoms, and attending to their emotional and spiritual needs. Within the United States the term is largely defined by the practices of the Medicare system and other health insurance providers, which make hospice care available, either in an inpatient facility or at the patient's home, to patients with a terminal prognosis who are medically certified to have less than six months to live. Outside the United States, the term hospice tends to be primarily associated with the particular buildings or institutions that specialise in such care (although so-called 'hospice at home' services may also be available).
Indemnity	An indemnity is a sum paid by A to B by way of compensation for a particular loss suffered by B.

16. THE FUTURE OF HEALTH CARE DELIVERY AND HEALTH POLICY

	The indemnifying party (A) may or may not be responsible for the loss suffered by the indemnified party (B). Forms of indemnity include cash payments, repairs, replacement, and reinstatement.
	In common parlance, indemnity is often used as a synonym for compensation or reparation.
Horizontal integration	In microeconomics and strategic management, the term horizontal integration describes a type of ownership and control. It is a strategy used by a business or corporation that seeks to sell a type of product in numerous markets. Horizontal integration in marketing is much more common than vertical integration is in production.
Information technology	Information Technology is the branch of engineering that deals with the use of computers and telecommunications to store, retrieve and transmit information.
Integrated delivery system	An integrated delivery system is a network of health care organizations under a parent holding company. Some Integrated delivery system have an HMO component, while others are a network of physicians only, or of physicians and hospitals. Thus, the term is used broadly to define an organization that provides a continuum of health care services.
Vertical integration	In microeconomics and management, the term vertical integration describes a style of management control. Vertically integrated companies in a supply chain are united through a common owner. Usually each member of the supply chain produces a different product or (market-specific) service, and the products combine to satisfy a common need.
Cranial root of accessory nerve	The cranial root of accessory nerve is the smaller of the two portions of the accessory nerve. It is generally considered as a part of the vagus nerve and not part of the accessory nerve proper because the cranial component rapidly joins the vagus nerve and serves the same function as other vagal nerve fibers.
	Its fibers arise from the cells of the nucleus ambiguus and emerge as four or five delicate rootlets from the side of the medulla oblongata, below the roots of the vagus.
Managed care	The term managed care is used in the United States to describe a variety of techniques intended to reduce the cost of providing health benefits and improve the quality of care ('managed care techniques') for organizations that use those techniques or provide them as services to other organizations ('managed care, or to describe systems of financing and delivering health care to enrollees organized around managed care techniques and concepts ('managed care delivery systems').

...intended to reduce unnecessary health care costs through a variety of mechanisms, including: economic incentives for physicians and patients to select less costly forms of care; programs for reviewing the medical necessity of specific services; increased beneficiary cost sharing; controls on inpatient admissions and lengths of stay; the establishment of cost-sharing incentives for outpatient surgery; selective contracting with health care providers; and the intensive management of high-cost health care cases. The programs may be provided in a variety of settings, such as Health Maintenance Organizations and Preferred Provider Organizations.

Public health	Public health is 'the science and art of preventing disease, prolonging life and promoting health through the organized efforts and informed choices of society, organizations, public and private, communities and individuals' (1920, C.E.A. Winslow). It is concerned with threats to health based on population health analysis. The population in question can be as small as a handful of people or as large as all the inhabitants of several continents (for instance, in the case of a pandemic).
Quality assurance	Quality assurance refers to administrative and procedural activities implemented in a quality system so that requirements and goals for a product, service or activity will be fulfilled. It is the systematic measurement, comparison with a standard, monitoring of processes and an associated feedback loop that confers error prevention. This can be contrasted with quality control, which is focused on process outputs.
Nurse Practitioner	A Nurse Practitioner is an Advanced Practice Nurse (APN) who has completed graduate-level education (either a Master's or a Doctoral degree). Additional APN roles include the Certified Registered Nurse Anesthetist (CRNA)s, CNMs, and CNSs. All Nurse Practitioners are Registered Nurses who have completed extensive additional education, training, and have a dramatically expanded scope of practice over the traditional RN role.
Intermountain Healthcare	Intermountain Health Care, Inc., officially doing business as as Intermountain Healthcare, is a non-profit healthcare system and is the largest healthcare provider in the Intermountain West. Until 2005 it known as Intermountain Health Care or more commonly IHC; it is now. Intermountain Healthcare is headquartered in Salt Lake City, Utah, and currently employs over 32,000 people.
Institution	An institution is any structure or mechanism of social order and cooperation governing the behavior of a set of individuals within a given human community. Institutions are identified with a social purpose and permanence, transcending individual human lives and intention by enforcing rules that governs cooperative human behavior. The term 'institution' is commonly applied to customs and behavior patterns important to a society, as well as to particular formal organizations of government and public service.

16. THE FUTURE OF HEALTH CARE DELIVERY AND HEALTH POLICY

Medical home	The medical home, is a team based health care delivery model led by a physician that provides comprehensive and continuous medical care to patients with the goal of obtaining maximized health outcomes (American College of Physicians) (American Academy of Family Physicians). It is 'an approach to providing comprehensive primary care for children, youth and adults'. The provision of medical homes may allow better access to health care, increase satisfaction with care, and improve health.
Palliative	Palliative care is an area of healthcare that focuses on relieving and preventing the suffering of patients. Unlike hospice care, palliative medicine is appropriate for patients in all disease stages, including those undergoing treatment for curable illnesses and those living with chronic diseases, as well as patients who are nearing the end of life. Palliative medicine utilizes a multidisciplinary approach to patient care, relying on input from physicians, pharmacists, nurses, chaplains, social workers, psychologists, and other allied health professionals in formulating a plan of care to relieve suffering in all areas of a patient's life.
Palliative care	Palliative care is an area of healthcare that focuses on relieving and preventing the suffering of patients. Unlike hospice care, palliative medicine is appropriate for patients in all disease stages, including those undergoing treatment for curable illnesses and those living with chronic diseases, as well as patients who are nearing the end of life. Palliative medicine utilizes a multidisciplinary approach to patient care, relying on input from physicians, pharmacists, nurses, chaplains, social workers, psychologists, and other allied health professionals in formulating a plan of care to relieve suffering in all areas of a patient's life.
Patient-centered medical home	The medical home, also known as the patient-centered medical home is a team based health care delivery model led by a physician, P.A., or N.P. that provides comprehensive and continuous medical care to patients with the goal of obtaining maximized health outcomes (American College of Physicians) (American Academy of Family Physicians). It is 'an approach to providing comprehensive primary care for children, youth and adults'. The provision of medical homes may allow better access to health care, increase satisfaction with care, and improve health.
Preferred provider organization	In health insurance in the United States, a preferred provider organization is a managed care organization of medical doctors, hospitals, and other health care providers who have covenanted with an insurer or a third-party administrator to provide health care at reduced rates to the insurer's or administrator's clients. Overview A preferred provider organization is a subscription-based medical care arrangement. A membership allows a substantial discount below the regularly charged rates of the designated professionals partnered with the organization.
Primary care	Primary care is the health care given by a health care provider. Typically this provider acts as the principal point of consultation for patients within a health care system and coordinates other specialists that the patient may need.

Public hospital	A public hospital is owned by a government and receives government funding. This type of hospital provides medical care free of charge, the cost of which is covered by the funding the hospital receives. Australia In Australia, public hospitals are operated and funded by each individual state's health department.
Resource-based relative value scale	Resource-based relative value scale is a schema used to determine how much money medical providers should be paid. It is partially used by Medicare in the United States and by nearly all Health maintenance organizations (HMOs). Resource based relative value scale assigns procedures performed by a physician or other medical provider a relative value which is adjusted by geographic region (so a procedure performed in Manhattan is worth more than a procedure performed in Dallas).
Risk	Risk is the potential that a chosen action or activity (including the choice of inaction) will lead to a loss (an undesirable outcome). The notion implies that a choice having an influence on the outcome sometimes exists . Potential losses themselves may also be called 'risks'.
Waterlow score	The 'Waterlow score gives an estimated risk of a patient developing a pressure sore. It is named after Judy Waterlow.
Joint Commission	The Joint Commission formerly the Joint Commission on Accreditation of Healthcare Organizations (JCAHO) and previous to that the Joint Commission on Accreditation of Hospitals (JCAH), is a United States-based nonprofit organization that accredits more than 19,000 health care organizations and programs in the United States. A majority of state governments have come to recognize Joint Commission accreditation as a condition of licensure and the receipt of Medicaid reimbursement. Surveys (inspections) typically follow a triennial cycle, with findings made available to the public in an accreditation quality report on the Quality Check Web site.
Socialized medicine	Socialized medicine is a term used in the United States to describe and discuss systems of universal health care - that is, medical and hospital care for all at a nominal cost by means of government regulation of health care and subsidies derived from taxation. Because of historically negative associations with socialism in American culture, the term is usually used pejoratively in American political discourse. The term was first widely used in the United States by advocates of the American Medical Association in opposition to President Harry S. Truman's 1947 health-care initiative.
Tertiary	The tertiary is a term for a geologic period 65 million to 1.8 million years ago. The tertiary covered the time span between the superseded Secondary period and an out-of-date definition of the Quaternary period.

16. THE FUTURE OF HEALTH CARE DELIVERY AND HEALTH POLICY

Tertiary care	In medicine, tertiary care is specialized consultative care, usually on referral from primary or secondary medical care personnel, by specialists working in a center that has personnel and facilities for special investigation and treatment. Examples of tertiary care services are specialist cancer care, neurosurgery (brain surgery), burns care and plastic surgery.
Coalition	A coalition is an alliance among individuals or groups, during which they cooperate in joint action, each in his own self-interest, joining forces together for a common cause. This alliance may be temporary or a matter of convenience. A coalition thus differs from a more formal covenant.
Initiative	An initiative represents an enterprise's readiness to embark on a new venture. Generally speaking, the motivation for an initiative arises from a desire to accomplish something that would benefit the enterprise, such as improving productivity, reducing costs or increasing market share. A typical initiative is expressed as a process and includes metrics and time frames.

1. _____ is a practice of protecting the natural environment on individual, organizational or governmental levels, for the benefit of the natural environment and humans. Due to the pressures of population and technology, the biophysical environment is being degraded, sometimes permanently. This has been recognized, and governments have begun placing restraints on activities that cause environmental degradation.

   a. Environmental law
   b. action plan
   c. Environmental protection
   d. Est: Playing the Game

2. . An _____ is an evolving concept defined as a systematic collection of electronic health information about individual patients or populations. It is a record in digital format that is theoretically capable of being shared across different health care settings. In some cases this sharing can occur by way of network-connected enterprise-wide information systems and other information networks or exchanges.

   a. Electronic medical record
   b. Enterprise master patient index
   c. Electronic health record

3. A _____ is an ancillary glyph added to a letter, 'distinguishing'). _____ is both an adjective and a noun, whereas diacritical is only an adjective.

   a. Diacritic
   b. NRC
   c. projective
   d. poor

4. In medicine, _____ refers to medical care not only of patients in the final hours or days of their lives, but more broadly, medical care of all those with a terminal illness or terminal condition that has become advanced, progressive and incurable.

   Regarding cancer care the United States National Cancer Institute writes:

   When a patient's health care team determines that the cancer can no longer be controlled, medical testing and cancer treatment often stop. But the patient's care continues.

   a. American Academy of Hospice and Palliative Medicine
   b. End-of-life care
   c. Ira Byock
   d. Interventionism

5. The _____ is the smaller of the two portions of the accessory nerve. It is generally considered as a part of the vagus nerve and not part of the accessory nerve proper because the cranial component rapidly joins the vagus nerve and serves the same function as other vagal nerve fibers.

   Its fibers arise from the cells of the nucleus ambiguus and emerge as four or five delicate rootlets from the side of the medulla oblongata, below the roots of the vagus.

   a. Neuroectoderm
   b. Paleocortex
   c. Cranial root of accessory nerve
   d. transduction